THE

7

INTUITIVE LAWS OF EMPLOYEE LOYALTY

Fascinating Truths About What It Takes to Create Truly Loyal and Engaged Employees

Heather R. Younger, J.D.

 LeadU
PUBLISHING

Since 2017

DENVER

Copyright © 2017 by LeadU Publishing. All rights reserved. Printed in the United States of America. Except as permitted under the United States Copyright Act of 1976, no part of this publication may be reproduced or distributed in any form or by any means, or stored in a database or retrieval system, without prior written of the publisher.

ISBN: 978-0-9990938-0-1

e-ISBN: 978-0-9990938-1-8

Library of Congress cataloging-in-Publication Data

Name: Younger, J.D., Heather, 1971-author.
Title: The 7 Intuitive Laws of Employee Loyalty: Fascinating Truths About What it Takes to Create Truly Loyal and Engaged Employees/ by Heather R. Younger, J.D.
Description: First Edition. | Colorado: LeadU Publications, 2017
Identifiers: Library of Congress 2017909143 | ISBN 9780999093801 (paperback) | ISBN
Subjects: Management, Leadership, Employee Engagement & Loyalty, Talent Management, Workplace Culture |BISAC: BUSINESS & ECONOMICS/Management

LeadU Publishing books are available at special quantity discounts to use as premium and sales promotions, or for use in corporate training programs. To contact a representative, please contact the author at (720) 295-1194.

TABLE OF CONTENTS

ACKNOWLEDGMENTS

I have many people who helped me get to where I am today. From an early age, I wanted to be an author and speaker. While I did not have a formal mentor, my grandmother, Ruth Gross, was my coach in many ways. She pushed me to want more and to be more. She would be proud.

To the nameless college professor who doubted I would ever go to law school. I thank you for being the fuel that I needed to achieve all that I set out to achieve. I won't say, "I told you so."

To my friends who believed in me along the way, thank you for being the inspiration to keep going. You give me faith in humankind.

My mother raised me to be the bigger person and treat everyone I meet with dignity and respect. I am a principled and empathetic person, because of her. Thank you, momma.

To my children, Gabriela, Sebastian, Dominic and Matteo. You inspire me to be better and leave a legacy. I love your strength and your unwavering belief in your faith. Thank you, too, for your patience with me when I could not always read to you at night, or spend extra time here and there. This book is a testament to your love for me.

To my husband, Luis, for being a strong source of consistency and love for our children. I would often be distracted by writing this book. You did not take it personally, but hunkered down to make sure we kept our home focused on our faith and our family. Thank you for being there for all of us.

Finally, to the Lord above. You made me to be the type of person who cares for others. You gave me the ability to speak up for others when others may fear doing so. Everything that is good in me is because you willed it so. Thank you!

AUTHOR'S NOTE

Many years ago, I attended law school. I admit that I loved it. The back and forth between the professors and the students was exhilarating! It was about the game of intellects. One of the first things we learned in law school was the idea of a contract. To have a viable contract, whether it be implied or explicit, there must be an offer, consideration and acceptance. Consideration means that the person accepting the offer had to give something in return for what was being offered. Once consideration was accepted, the contract was considered final. This is what is referred to as "Meeting of the Minds."

I have not practiced law for some time now. As you can imagine, people often ask me if I would ever practice law again, and I confess to them that the only area of law that ever really intrigued me was employment law. I realized early on in my working career that there was a real imbalance between employees and the organizations that employ them.

During my career, I saw that many organizational leaders failed to ask employees what they thought and often ignored what they heard from employees anyway. I became a natural sounding board for staff and worked to communicate a compelling message to those leaders who determined organizational direction and culture.

On a very personal note, and my "why" for writing this book: I felt undervalued, unheard, and unimportant when I was a child. I am the product of an interracial and interfaith home. My mother was from an Orthodox Jewish home, and my father was a non-practicing Christian and African American. My mother's parents were not happy at all that my mother and father got married. Unfortunately, they let us know of their displeasure in subtle and not-so-subtle ways. I was never included in family functions. I was hidden from family and community friends. I was often voiceless, although I walked around pretending that everything was just fine.

It was not fine. No one thought to ask me how I felt or what I needed. Whether I wanted to be included as a full member of the family was not left for me to decide. I was an outsider. In a paradoxical twist, it was my mother's mother who pushed me to go to law school. I held a very naïve subconscious belief that my attending law school would elevate me in the eyes of the family. My grandmother wanted me to be her "little lawyer," but she did not want anyone else to know I was the product of a perceived failure on her part.

I realized early on that I needed to speak clearly and confidently. I needed to use the power I gained from becoming an educated person to begin to chart my own course. To this day, my strengths of empathy, relatability, and communication come from my struggle to belong inside my own family. I realized, too, the importance of having a voice and using it to persuade others to act for their benefit and mine. I have represented clients in court. I have advocated for customers and employees alike. This is because I was gifted to empathize with, relate to, and communicate with others. Often, employees do not feel heard. They feel undervalued and undermined just like I did.

I found my way out of that by using my gifts to highlight the disconnect to organizational leaders. I am able to communicate an authentic employee voice to those who can make change happen. This is why I am writing this book, and this is why I do what I do.

INTRODUCTION

Employees are loyal to organizations that have great people who care.

Loyalty is defined as "a strong feeling of support or allegiance."
I will come back to this important point soon.

I will use employees, teammates, and workforce interchangeably
throughout the book as they mean the same thing.

This book is both strategic and practical. I write using big themes and
then narrow the concepts down into stories and then principles that
reinforce the contract. If you are reading this book, it means that you
are interested in retaining engaged and loyal employees. You may even
be frustrated by what appears to be uncontrolled turnover of
top talent.

My hope for you after reading this book is that you will:

1. Come away refreshed in the key principles of what it takes
   to retain top talent (for much longer than you think).

2. Be clear about the role your thoughts and actions play in
   creating an engaging workplace that attracts and keeps
   the best people.

3. Become motivated to take some of the steps suggested
   in this book.

When I refer to "organizational leaders" or "organizations," I am
referring to C-level executives, boards, human resource executives,
and operational leaders. Organizations are made up of people, not just
corporate structures, processes and systems. Organizational leaders are
the ones primarily responsible for setting and affirming organizational
behaviors. I do not mean to imply that frontline employees have no
ownership in their own engagement. I believe just the opposite.
Primarily, though, this is a handbook for leaders both inside and
outside of human resources who want to proactively create
more-loyal employees.

In true "Voice of the Employee" fashion, I have included "readers' comments" that I took from articles I wrote over the years. There is no better way to get to the bottom of this important topic than to let employees from around the world chime in.

Finally, I hope that you do not take my writing style to be preachy. To the contrary, I long for all leaders to keep doing what they are doing to promote a positive work culture where employees feel valued, respected, listened to and important. My wish for those who read it is that they feel the heart that is present in its words.

LOVE THE ONES YOU HAVE

Employees are a company's greatest asset – they're your competitive advantage. You want to attract and retain the best; provide them with encouragement, stimulus, and make them feel that they are an integral part of the company's mission.

ANNE MULCAHY

We have all heard the "employee first, customer second" philosophy of growing and maintaining a flourishing business. Here are some concrete reasons why business leaders would want to live and breathe this mindset into their organizations.

Side note: Smart business leaders are really working with both stakeholders simultaneously, focusing on building trust, rapport, and alliances with both. So, the true meaning of this approach is not to stop answering your customers' phone calls or meeting their needs until you get your relationship with your employees "just right." It is meant to signal to internal and external customers alike that you understand that you cannot give what you do not have.

Employees Will Go The Extra Mile

I have found that employees who feel cared for and those who feel empowered to make decisions that benefit customers and the organization are much more likely to go the extra mile for customers and for the business.

I once worked with a team member who had been at the organization for 20 years. This particular person came in at 6:30 every morning and would often be found leaving around the same time at night.

She would not leave until customers were satisfied and her job had been done. One clear example of her going the extra mile was a time when a large customer's order was about to ship, and she realized that it was inaccurate. She did not spend a lot of time figuring out who did it or placing blame elsewhere. (We did this after solving the immediate issue.) She took ownership for the result and decided to come in on a weekend to work with the shipping department to make sure the correct order was shipped to the customer.

She did not walk away until she had a satisfied, loyal customer.

An organization cannot buy this type of commitment to excellence. It must be earned.

Employees Are A More Affordable Source Of Promotion

One thing I know for sure. I would be a lot less likely to "talk up" a current employer if I did not feel like the leaders cared about me, by investing resources in my development or by ensuring I had a voice and a way to be a part of organizational change. Many would have a hard time being the cheerleader for a company that shuts down input, treats them like a number, and fails to recognize their efforts.

The flip side of this is that putting the employee first ensures any organization a more affordable source of promotion to anyone who wants to listen. Employees who are deeply engaged in the work they do usually spread the news to customers, friends, family, and anyone else who will listen. Harness this continuous energy!

Employees Refer Other Great Employees

Do you think that a 5-star employee is going to refer a 2-star employee to your organization? Not very likely.

Employees who have worked for a significant period of time for an organization, and who take ownership in the success of the organization usually refer like-minded people to open positions.

If the organization takes care of its people, those same people will reach down deep to refer their most experienced and respected friends and former colleagues to fill key positions in the organization. These referrals are a reflection of the employees' deeper commitment to the company, its brand and its culture. Never underestimate the value of the "Employee First" philosophy in strengthening your talent acquisition strategy.

Employees Sell More Stuff

Much has been written about how engaged and loyal employees will drive increased revenues for an organization. This is certainly not a new concept, but I think the real question should be "why?" We can all guess the reasons why this is, but I would propose that the reason is very basic. It really stems from the notion of reciprocity.

Reciprocity is the quality or state of being reciprocal:
mutual dependence, action, or influence
MERRIAM WEBSTER DICTIONARY

You see, an employee who feels as though his/her employer has provided the tangible and intangible benefits that makes the relationship one of trust and co-creation tends to want to reciprocate. That employee may then act in a way, like selling more goods and services (even if this is not his/her role), to "return the favor."
This is what leads to mutual dependence or influence.

Organizations should want to create this type of feeling in their employees. Once they do, the sky is the limit!

In the end, considering the unique psychological contract that exists between an organization and its employees, putting employees first is just the right thing to do in every situation. Customers will sense this mutual commitment, and this affects their loyalty to the organization as well.

ROI OF EMPLOYEE ENGAGEMENT AND LOYALTY

Higher workplace engagement leads to 37% lower absenteeism, 41% fewer safety incidents, and 41% fewer quality defects.

Highly engaged employees are:

- 2.5 times more likely to stay at work late if something needs to be done after the normal workday ends.

- More than twice as likely to help someone at work even if they ..... don't ask for help.

- More than three times as likely to do something good for the company that is not expected of them.

- More than five times as likely to recommend that a friend or relative apply for a job at their company.

CONSEQUENCES OF NOT HAVING LOYAL EMPLOYEES

So why is it important that organizations even care about employee loyalty? To some, employees get paid a wage, and they need to just do their jobs and grin and bear it. Why is it such a big deal to be thinking about creating loyal employees? What's in it for you?

Gallup found that companies that increase their number of talented managers and double the rate of engaged employees achieve, on average, 147% higher earnings per share than their competition.

High Turnover And Increased Costs Of Recruitment

This is an intuitive point, but the cost to recruit new employees after those you have already developed leave is astronomical.

Here are some scary statistics:

- Each year the average company loses 20-50% of its employee base

- Cost of replacing entry level employees: 30-50% of their annual salary

- Cost of replacing mid-level employees: 150% of their annual salary

- Millennial turnover costs the U.S. economy $30.5 billion annually.

- The cost of replacing high-level or highly specialized employees: 400% of their annual salary.

The point here is that organizations pay a huge price for not putting employee retention strategies in place that will stop talented employees from walking out the door.

Effect On Culture

Organizations are made up of people. Those people work and "live" there with other people at least 40 hours per week. Like the connective tissue that begins to form when we are injured or when we are healing and becomes a part of who we are, team members are a part of the connective tissue of the organization.

What happens when we remove or tear out a piece of that tissue? Not only does it hurt a lot, it causes heavy bleeding. If it doesn't heal properly, there are complications. We may never regain our function in that area. When good productive people leave, we feel the pain and so does the culture of the team. The only way to mend the tissue permanently is to do the right things to engage and retain them.

Spillover Effect

We don't talk about this much, but there is a psychological impact on other productive and engaged employees when they are forced to work with disengaged employees. Whether it is during water cooler talk or just in combined work spaces, the negative energy that disengaged employees pass to the entire team and organization can be toxic.

Oftentimes, the disengaged employees are the scapegoats to deeper organizational issues. When we do not look at what is causing them to be disengaged, we enable the spillover effect to continue. Organizations that want a thriving workplace must rid themselves of disengaged employees, not necessarily by termination, but by living by the Laws found in this book.

Negative Word Of Mouth

Remember that unhappy employees don't make for good promoters of your brand. In fact, disengaged employees are likely to tell more people and blurt it out all over social media and at every party. Reputationally, this negative word of mouth works against your brand promise.

Who are you out in the world to your customers? Whatever that is, it must match who you are to your employees.

Loss Of Organizational Stability

Stop for a minute and think about what it says to your customers, partners, and investors when your employees keep walking out the door. Potentially, they could be in the middle of a complex project implementation and having a consistent point of contact through that process is key.

I can tell you from experience that you can only hide your retention issues so long before the external world uncovers them and they start to impact those relationships and the bottom line. Customers want to work with stable organizations that they know will be around to back up their promises for great products and services. Employee loyalty plays a huge role in this regard.

BRING THE RIGHT ONES IN THE DOOR

Providing a positive candidate experience can be a major differentiator in the market too many companies do not understand the importance of it they skip to hire without putting thought into what leads up to that.

(READER COMMENT)

Before I delve into the Laws of employee loyalty, it is important to tackle the issue of candidate recruitment and consider the role that the candidate experience plays in fostering or detracting from employee loyalty.

A while back, I watched *Draft Day* with Kevin Costner. I would not ordinarily watch a show about the draft process in the NFL, but my husband was very persuasive and thought I would find some nuggets in it.

He was right!

At the 30,000-foot level, most of the movie focused on what takes place from the emotional perspective on the side of the prospective NFL picks and the general managers (GMs) who must consider which team members to bring aboard. It was a roller coaster ride, to say the least.

While the film highlighted much of the politics that exist in the process, it also made quite clear that the process of player selection is very complicated. On one hand, there were players who were very hard workers with tons of integrity and who wanted to be on the top team, because it felt right and they knew their talents would be best served there. There were also those who simply just wanted to "get paid" and be superstars.

On the GM side of things, it was clear that the player with the top stats was not necessarily the player who would be selected in the first round, especially if there were other intangible characteristics that might detract from team cohesion.

In talent acquisition and talent management, leaders are often faced with some of these same intersections. There are candidates who really want to be at an organization, because they feel it is the right place for them to be for a variety of reasons. They may not have all the requisite experience based upon the job posting, but they have desire, passion, and tenacity.

In some cases, there are candidates who make it easy for recruiters to check off the bullet points of a job posting, but lack in the areas of passion, culture alignment, or any other intangible attribute. If all the stars align, one candidate might possess it all.

The GM in *Draft Day* had to balance his desire to get the "winner" based upon everyone else's perception and his gut feeling to recruit very strong players with integrity, passion, strong leadership skills, and the ability to foster team cohesion. Similarly, talent acquisition leaders struggle to choose employees who really want to be there for the right reasons.

Talent acquisition and talent management, then, become two sides of the same coin. Just as it boils down to character and culture fit when selecting great candidates, the same attributes are key to move the organization forward.

It is equally important for candidates to feel that they are going to work with or are working for an organizational leader who has integrity and that will focus on creating a culture where all employees feel important and engaged.

So, the question then becomes in the minds of prospective, current, and future team members, how much do you want me? What are you prepared to do to get me, keep me, and make me love you so much, I will refer equally aligned future employees your way?

I hypothesize that what it takes to land the "best" candidates is also what it takes to keep the best employees for the long haul.

MEETING OF THE MINDS

People are not "the company's greatest asset," they ARE the company. Companies are not a disconnected set of products and policies but an organization of people with ideals, plans, passions. So many leaders seek to understand the culture of their company and try to change it through policy and vision and fail to invest in the people that inform and build the culture.

(READER COMMENT)

Back to the idea of "Meeting of the Minds." I learned early on in law school that no matter what an employer or employee thinks they owe to the other, it is the other party's belief about what they think you owe them that creates a disconnect. It is how they measure their loyalty to you. The size of the gap is what determines their length of stay with your organization.

This is the foundation for the psychological contract that exists between employer and employee, which is defined as:

" representing the mutual beliefs, perceptions, and informal obligations between an employer and an employee. It sets the dynamics for the relationship and defines the detaile practicality of the work to be done. It is distinguishable from the formal written contract of employment which, for the most part, only identifies mutual duties and responsibilities in a generalized form." Rousseau, D. M. (1989). Psychological and implied contracts in organizations. Employee Responsibilities and Rights Journal, 2: 121-139.

While I will focus on the feelings and needs of employees, this contract is mutual and does require a look at both sides of the relationship. The idea of a psychological contract is very philosophical, but I also believe that we must understand the history, the "why" and the big picture behind what drives employees to become and stay engaged and what contributes to them staying longer with organizations. This will be the fundamental focus of this book.

In *The Alliance: Managing Talent in the Networked Age*, Hoffman, Casnocha, and Yeh lay out the idea that employer and employee expectations have greatly changed. They remind us that as late as a decade ago, employees stayed forever, but this has changed. When businesses began to focus more on making outside stakeholders happy financially, employees became an afterthought.

The authors of The Alliance posit that frequent checkpoints create a perfect scenario where employer and employee sit down to openly discuss their expectations, to calibrate where the other wants to go and to fill any gaps that may have developed along the way.

How can organizations try to align this meeting of the minds from the beginning? Be more explicit in your expectations and offerings. What if they are existing employees? How do they realign with longer- term employees? What can they do to minimize a breach in the psychological contract with new employees? Build in processes to ensure that calibration is balanced. The Laws found in the following pages will help leaders answer these questions.

Organizational leaders must continue to focus on the journey while never resting on their laurels. The move to create more-loyal employees is a process, and it does not happen overnight. Great talent may leave along the way, but the journey is still worth it.

When we keep in mind that the psychological contract drives employee and employer expectations, we can then see how any deficiencies in how employers meet those expectations can directly impact employee loyalty. This book is not as much focused on how to keep employees for a lifetime as it is focused on retaining them longer than they would ordinarily stay and turning them into brand advocates for future recruiting efforts.

THE SUM OF ITS PARTS

I looked at seven intuitive Laws that employers can follow to extend the ordinary stay of employees and to maximize their time with the organization. Please do not be literal about how I organized the chapters. They are not necessarily in order of importance. In fact, some are more important than others depending upon the organization, the strategic goals, timing for employees, and so on. There is one caveat; the first law is Give them great supportive managers. This was purposefully placed, because none of the other Laws matter if organizations don't abide by the laws of leadership. This is also one of the more robust chapters of the book. The remaining chapters are organized, highlighting these seven intuitive Laws. You will also notice that I have inserted "contract reinforcement" principles in different areas of the book. These are meant to provide you with specific action steps to help bring the bigger picture to life.

The book is organized using the following seven Laws:

1. Give them great supportive managers

2. Recognize your employees often

3. Give them a voice and do something about it

4. Grow and promote their talents

5. Foster deep connections with and in them

6. Make team the focus

7. Pay them equitably

A GIFT FOR YOU

In order to help you keep these Laws front and center in your personal workplace, I created a colorful infographic with all of the Laws on it. My hope is that you will be reminded of what is necessary as a leader to create a more loyal team. Print it out in color and laminate it. Better yet, provide a copy to all your team leaders.

GO TO CUSTOMERFANATIX.COM/RESOURCES TO ACCESS YOUR COPY.

THE 7 INTUITIVE LAWS OF EMPLOYEE LOYALTY

LAW #1 GIVE THEM GREAT SUPPORTIVE MANAGERS

"WHILE GOOD MANAGERS CAN BE CREATED, GREAT MANAGERS USUALLY POSSESS NATURAL TENDENCIES THAT MAKE THEM GREAT."

RECOGNIZE 79% OF EMPLOYEES

LAW #2 YOUR EMPLOYEES OFTEN

LAW #3 GIVE THEM A VOICE!

WHO QUIT THEIR JOBS CITE A LACK OF APPRECIATION AS A KEY REASON FOR LEAVING.'

"EMPLOYEES FEEL VALUED & SUCCESSFUL WHEN THEY FEEL THEIR VOICE IS HEARD. NOT ONLY THAT, THEY FEEL LIKE A VESTED MEMBER OF THE ORGANIZATIONS WHEN, AT LEAST, SOME OF THEIR VOICE LEADS TO POSITIVE CHANGE."

GROW & PROMOTE
THEIR TALENT

LAW #4 **78%** SAID THEY WOULD REMAIN LONGER WITH THEIR EMPLOYER IF THEY SAW A CAREER PATH WITH THE CURRENT ORGANIZATION.'

LAW #5 FOSTER DEEP CONNECTIONS WITH THEM

"ONE OF THE BIGGEST FAILURES THAT MANAGERS MAKE IS TO EXPECT GREAT THINGS FROM THEIR TEAM MEMBERS WITHOUT FIRST SETTING A COMPELLING VISION FOR THEM TO FOLLOW."

MAKE TEAMWORK THE FOCUS
LAW #6

MANAGERS ACCOUNT FOR AT LEAST 70% OF VARIANCE IN EMPLOYEE ENGAGEMENT SCORES ACROSS BUSINESS UNITS. WHEN IT COMES TO ENGAGING EMPLOYEES AND MEETING THEIR NEEDS, GREAT MANAGERS CAN BE THE KEY TO UNLOCKING HIGH PERFORMANCE.'

LAW #7 PAY THEM EQUITABLY

JUST 37% OF ENGAGED EMPLOYEES WOULD CONSIDER LEAVING FOR A 20% RAISE OR LESS, COMPARED TO 54% OF ACTIVELY DISENGAGED EMPLOYEES.'

LAW #1

GIVE THEM GREAT

SUPPORTIVE MANAGERS

*The main factor in workplace discontent is not wages,
benefits, or hours, but the boss.*

HBR, 2015

This fact that is undisputed. A manager can make or break employee loyalty. I start with this Law, because it has the most impact on the way employees feel about their job and about the organization for which they work. All other Laws are secondary to this one. It will outline the ways managers can leverage their power to reinforce the psychological contract and live up to their end of the bargain.

THE MAKEUP OF A GREAT MANAGER

Whom companies name as manager is one of the most important decisions they make given that managers play a critical role in driving engagement in any organization. Whether hiring from the outside or promoting from within, organizations that scientifically select managers for the unique talents it takes to effectively manage people greatly increase the odds of employee engagement.

It has become painfully clear to me that many managers need extensive development in how to engage their team members. Unfortunately, many either do not have the time or do not want to make the time to improve in this area. The worst of them don't see themselves as needing improvement!

Managers who fail to listen to their team, fail to help their team members reach professional goals, show very little in the way of caring for each member of their team, and often work against the team are the primary reasons why employees quit. As such, it is critical that organizations get the manager hiring and selection process down to a science. While good managers can be created, great managers usually possess natural tendencies that make them great.

I have worked for the good, great, and not-so-great managers. I can say without a doubt that the great managers really focused a lot of their time on engaging and developing their teams. The relationship and connection between manager and employee cannot be understated when it comes to engagement.

Dictionary.com defines **manager** as:

> " a person who has control or direction of an institution, business, etc., or of a part, division, or phase of it."

Sounds like a *respectable* thing to do, don't you think?

Sadly, the word "manager" has become like a four-letter word and downright offensive to some. It used to be that being a manager was a position we all wanted to reach. People used to aspire to be a manager in their field of choice. Now, when we use the word manager, people tend to cringe due to thoughts of some very bad experiences.

We can use the word "leader" here as well.

Dictionary.com defines **leader** as:

> " a person or thing that leads, a guiding or directing head, as of an army, movement, or political group."

Both *manager* and *leader* have an element of directing, but the *leader* also "guides". Nonetheless, employees refer to leaders as "my manager," or "my boss." I think that managers can hold a respectable place again and thus chose to use the word manager in this Law.

The remaining elements of this Law will highlight the key attributes of a great supportive manager.

PUT THEIR NEEDS ABOVE YOUR OWN

Employees are disposable commodities to most companies.
They can be dispensed with at any time to make the directors a bonus
and are the first casualties of any "strategy" to reduce cost. Never give up
your personal life for a company. You will get no thanks. They will cover
their own backsides before they will protect yours.

(READER COMMENT)

I have managed and been managed, I have led, and been led by great leaders and horrible managers alike. The worst managers are those with a tremendous amount of ego. The best leaders often have a sense of selflessness and the need to bring out the best in others. Just watch in your own office environment, employees will talk amongst themselves about so and so...you know that one employee who goes out of their way to help everybody else, that's your best person for the job.

Employees are people. While they want to know that you care for them, they also want to know that when the rubber hits the road you will put their needs first.

They can see right through any insincerity, and they know when you are putting your needs above theirs. They know if you are covering your own backside. Show them you care by letting them know that you are interested in them outside of what they can do for you, or how they can help you move up the career ladder. If it is not about more than that, very few employees will remain loyal to organizations that are not loyal to them.

GIVE THEM YOUR UNDIVIDED ATTENTION

I learned early on in my management career that I could achieve more with a team than I could by myself. Having said that, the most important tactical thing I ever instituted as a leader was to set one-on-one meetings every single week with my team members. (Some of you may cringe at the thought of having to set aside so much time while having to wear many other hats, but I promise you that you will not regret doing this.) I highly recommend this to a leader who is looking to take the team or a division to the next level. People will say much more about their fears, goals, and desires in a meeting alone with their manager than they will in a crowded room.

While I still think that team meetings are key for cohesiveness, the dividends that a manager earns by investing the time to privately meet each direct report is crucial.

COACH THEM TO COURSE-CORRECT WITH LOVE

I know the word "love" used in the work environment makes some feel a little uneasy (and conjures up images I apologize for bringing to the surface), but we spend many of our waking hours with people with whom we work. When I say that I love my team members, what I am really saying is that I have a huge amount of respect for them as individuals and that I long for them to grow and for me to grow while coaching them to become their best. I am a caring manager.

I do not want you to think that managing a team is all about flowers and chirping birds. Occasionally, I have found it necessary to sit down with a team member to help them course-correct. There may have been something they said in a team meeting, or a way in which they spoke to a customer. Whatever the reason, I always chose to coach out of love.

This type of discussion usually ends with some good insight and next steps. The purpose is to help them uncover alternative paths that may produce more fruitful results. Because they know immediately whether you are a caring manager, they appreciate the time you invest in them.

INITIATE CONSISTENT PROFESSIONAL DEVELOPMENT TALKS

This is not the same as recognition for specific efforts or results. When a manager chooses to speak with team members regarding their professional development, this tells the team member that no matter how many course-correction discussions they have had, the manager still wants to invest time in developing them.

It shows the team that they are more than just employees; they are people you care about in and of themselves and not for your own gain. This is hugely meaningful to anyone who is on the other end. It may be a conversation about a possible position opening up that will mean a promotion for them and a shift out of your department. You are focused on their advancement and growth. If you do not do this already, try it. Even if they decide not to pursue the path you discussed, they will respect you and appreciate you even more for going down that road with them.

MEET THEM WHERE THEY ARE

A while back, I watched "Sister Act 2" with my kiddos. It is one of the few movies that all four of my kids will sit down and watch with me. While it has some far-fetched ideas in it, it has some powerful lessons to inspire even the toughest of skin.

There is the all-too-familiar-but-never-tiring scene where the music teacher, played by Whoopi Goldberg, who is pretending to be a nun, realizes that she has some very talented music students. She does not try to fit them into some type of square peg and make them sing things that do not interest them. Instead, she meets them where they are and uses their love of Rap and R&B music to ignite an unquenchable passion in all of them. It all culminates with these previously uninspired and underprivileged teens becoming the best gospel/hip hop Catholic-school choir there ever was.

I admit it is a little corny, but I like corny. The times when I am most inspired are when something that I thought would never in a million years happen does indeed happen. I live my life by the possibilities that exist in the world not yet defined by anyone. Thinking back on my long career as a customer-facing leader, I was most successful when I met my customers where they were. I focused on what inspired them and how I could ignite that inspiration in order to keep them engaged and retain them. Employees are no different.

A client of mine recalled working with an employee who had a reputation for being grumpy and the-glass-is-half-empty kind of thinker. She had a hard time convincing him that he needed to change his attitude and become more service-focused. She decided to meet him where he was and turn this attitude into a running joke that then made him start to think of himself as that person every time he walked into her office.

He became more aware. Over time, he would go out of his way to prove that he could be different. It was not going to be an overnight transformation. Nonetheless, that manager continued to meet him where he was, calling him on the carpet when he regressed to his old ways, but recognizing his effort to change. It had an impact.

Leaders who focus on meeting their teammates where they are and find ways to inspire the greatness within them will have crazy success in keeping them for the long haul and getting plenty of good employee referrals along the way.

CONTRACT REINFORCEMENT

What can you do today as a leader of teams to meet your team members where they are? Find out what makes each team member get excited, or think through a message that resonates with them, and use that to communicate necessary performance improvements or recognize their efforts.

BE VULNERABLE

As a team leader or manager, so many feel that they need to put too much "professional distance" between colleagues or employees, which prevents genuine dialogue and connection. By being available and in touch with your team, you not only keep them engaged with you, you keep them engaged with their work, the company, and help resolve issues before they become concerns or problems. People respond to a leader who cares about them and demonstrates a positive attitude about their work, not just someone who drops a project or direction in their lap and walks away. Compassion is so relevant in leadership within today's business marketplace.

(READER COMMENT)

We often think of leaders as strong and confident individuals who possess or show very few faults. I would argue that we should turn this idea of leadership on its head. Vulnerable leaders are more beloved. Show more of yourself if you want to connect with and retain your team members.

Employees follow vulnerable leaders. They prefer to be in the trenches with a leader who shows that they do not have to be perfect in order to do great things.

Think about the managers you respect most. Aren't they the ones that occasionally poke fun of themselves or have a certain amount of transparency?

This is an attractive trait to have as a leader and a manager, because it makes taking risks and falling short acceptable. This is when things get fun!

We must be willing to follow in order to effectively lead. It can become a barrier to team and organizational greatness when leaders pretend that everything is golden. Your team is attuned to your mood swings (no matter how much you hide them). While you don't have to reveal every piece of dirty laundry, your team should see some of the good and bad. This is how they measure you as a leader.

How do you show up? How do you handle setbacks?

This can be difficult to do for many, but we can never really gain our team's respect without revealing that we are human and mess up sometimes. Employees are drawn to leaders who don't fear appearing imperfect. A team will never really grow to be fruitful without this important ingredient.

BE HUMBLE

As leaders, we all have a tendency to get a little stuffy once in a while. Consequently, appearing superior to the team we support does nothing but put distance between us, the frontline, and the customer. Do you ever struggle with being more human and approachable?

Try to maintain heightened awareness of your presence and whether you are bringing people toward you. When you are more purposeful in your humility and setting yourself up to be with your people, they will feel more connected to you and the organization.

The result?

More connectedness means that they will be more willing to put forth extra effort, which can pay off in increased profits and increased retention.

SAY HELLO AND GOODBYE

I have to say this one seems to get the most whispers and negative comments with the frontline. This may seem very obvious, but walking past frontline employees without saying hello or goodbye is a major mistake. Failing to do this one basic thing is one of the biggest reasons why employees feel disconnected from organizational leadership. This would also make them wonder whether you know their name or even care.

I once worked with a manager who knew that he was leaving his team's potential on the table for his lack of recognizing them in the most basic way. He noticed that his unit's performance was much lower than his colleagues'. When he took ownership in creating deeper connection with them, he began to see the changes in them and in their numbers.

CONTRACT REINFORCEMENT

Start tracking every day that you say hello to just one of your team members, then make sure to start and greet others too. You will make them feel like valuable members of the team and not just a number.

GIVE SOME AWAY

I get it.

You have a job to do and want to be moving forward and, most likely, upward. Take some time to think about how you can give away some of your power, authority, or influence to key members of your team. I am not saying that you let everyone run rampant with no sense of who owns what. Rather, let your team have a chance to lead even if it puts you in the backseat.

When your employees feel empowered to do good work and grow in and around their current role, you will hold their attention longer. Never assume that where they are in their current role is where they want to end up.

INCLUDE THEM

Not in all cases, but in many cases, employees feel stifled because change happens all around them and they are not involved in it, nor are they aware of how they are connected to it.
Leaders may feel that they do not "need" to tell their team (or organization) about every initiative before it becomes real. While I agree that too much can just be too much, it is very important to have a communication strategy around significant organizational or departmental changes.

Have you ever been on the tail end of an organizational change and you were the last to find out?

Then you are expected to embrace it wholeheartedly?

How did that make you feel?

Some of the greatest managers take the time to sit down with their teams and share organizational changes. Better yet, they take the time to listen to employee concerns and solicit feedback. This act makes them feel safe and cared for. This type of treatment is completely in line with the psychological contract, because it meets the employees' basic expectation that they be informed about decisions that affect them.

CONTRACT REINFORCEMENT

Form some type of frontline employee committee to serve in an advisory function for you. They can give you great insights into how to move forward with the initiative and can enlist more champions to communicate and excite others.

BE TRANSPARENT

One of my colleagues told me a story of when he was set to present on a huge project plan that he was assigned. His manager was aware that the budget had been adjusted for this particular project, but chose not to tell my colleague of the budget reduction. So when my colleague went to present the project plan to the project committee, they all had that deer caught in the headlights look about them. What my colleague did not know until then was that his budget figures were way off in the wrong direction. He was mortified!

Later, he found out that his manager knew this before he went into the meeting, but let him look like a fool. As a result, he never trusted that manager again and began to look for work elsewhere. This is a red flag for most employees. Most employees quit their managers, not their organizations. Transparency leads to trust. Trust is the foundation for a healthy psychological contract.

Picture this: Your boss tells you that you have to increase productivity by 30% and reduce expenses by 20% by the end of the quarter, or you will be forced to roll out a furlough plan. Immediately after concluding that little talk with your boss, you run into a staff meeting with an apparent scowl on your face. Everyone asks you what is bothering you and you say something like, "Nothing at all. Everything is fine." You think that you are being a good leader by not sharing your experience with your team. Do you know what you did? You have just increased your team's anxiety, broken down bonds of trust, and shown them that you do not think they can handle the truth.

From my experiences with managing teams in different settings, I have discovered that transparent leaders are much more effective at building loyal and cohesive teams than those who attempt to keep information close to their vests. As far as leadership qualities go, transparency is a differentiator.

Below are the key reasons why leaders who lack transparency have difficulty retaining loyal followers:

Create Anxiety

The Dalai Lama once said, "A lack of transparency results in distrust and a deep sense of insecurity." When a leader makes a conscious decision to hide the truth, and instead paints the picture that everything is just peachy, the team experiences anxiety and insecurity about the status of their jobs and or the perceived quality of their work. However, if we reframe the opening scene to one where the leader walks into a staff meeting shortly after speaking to her boss and the team asks what's bothering her, she then might say something like, "I am a little distracted. I just left a meeting with John and he set some pretty aggressive targets for our team by the end of the quarter. I would like to turn this meeting into a brainstorming session around how we will all pitch in to meet these new aggressive goals. How does that sound?" Now, the team may experience some initial anxiety after hearing this, but now the team has been armed with the knowledge and would be empowered to come up with a joint plan.

Break Down Trust

Jack Welch wrote in his book, *Winning*, that "candor unclutters." What he meant by this is that transparency and candor build deep trust between people. The best leaders know that trust is the currency required to inspire a team to new heights. If lofty goals are put in front of a team with a transparent leader, the team members will willingly follow because they know that there are no secrets. If the leader chooses to hide things from the team, the team will always question the leader's intentions and integrity. Ultimately, the team will question whether the leader has their best interests in mind.

Hinder Collaboration

Once an enlightened leader decides to become transparent, the team members will almost immediately start to take on joint accountability and collaborate on solutions to a disclosed problem or goal. It is a fallacy that all leaders must go quietly into the night and take the world on their shoulders alone. While this is partly true, it is not wholly necessary. Once a leader embraces the idea that transparency will improve the position and bond of the team, the leader will know that they are not in it alone.

CONTRACT REINFORCEMENT

Commit to stop holding information so tightly to your vest. Open up and solicit feedback from your team. Let them help you solve the problem. You will be pleasantly surprised by the results!

BELIEVE IN THEM

If your actions inspire others to dream more, learn more, do more and become more, you are a leader.

JOHN QUINCY ADAMS

I have always believed that my role as a leader was to help my team believe in themselves and their unlimited potential. There have been many times when a team member has come to me with great doubt over a course of action they were trying to take. I could always see it in their eyes. There are so many business quotes and articles about believing in ourselves. This is a critical point for self-esteem. Equally as important is a manager's ability to inspire their team members to do great things just by believing in them.

I am not saying that I believe that we can all become the President of the United States and push people in that direction. That would be plain hard-headed and unrealistic. Nonetheless, our goal should always be to help set a vision for each individual that complements their talents and gifts and encourage them to see the possibilities more clearly.

CASE IN POINT

Many years ago, I worked my way up in Mary Kay Cosmetics (yes, a lawyer who was selling cosmetics). To this day, it was the best career journey I took. For me, the best thing was working with women who overcame self-doubt, tried new things, and oftentimes flourished. Witnessing them bloom was amazing, feeling as though my belief in them helped felt good too.

One consultant who is still near and dear to my heart joined the company, because she believed in the message of financial freedom and helping other women grow into self-driven leaders. She wanted to be successful as a new consultant. She wanted that pink Cadillac. Fundamentally, she longed for someone to believe in her. She wanted someone to invest in her to help her be her very best self. Coupled with her self-doubt, there were bits of confidence. She was coming out of her cocoon. It was beautiful!

I still think of her. Although she never "made it big" in Mary Kay, I always believed that she could. She didn't win the Cadillac, or big awards, but she tried damn hard to. She gained a lot more confidence too.

She reminds me of so many team members and managers who only need someone to believe in them. If you have the desire to leave your permanent footprint at home, in your workplace, or in this world, I would highly recommend that you believe in others.

Yes. This can be dangerous, or even a huge let-down if they fall short of meeting your image of them. That is all right. I promise you that you will remember those let-downs much less when you continue to believe and see the positive impact you have on others' lives. Look for that glimmer!

PUTTING THE DOT ON THE "I" IN BELIEVE

I have four young children, so I watch a lot of children's movies. The movies often teach me lessons. Charlotte's Web was no exception. Charlotte's Web is a story about a pig and his touching friendship with a spider. For a family movie, it had many complex relationship concepts Admittedly, I shed the occasional tear while watching it.

The overarching storyline goes like this: The pig lives on a farm where he becomes a dear friend to the other animals. The other animals and Charlotte, the spider, realize what happens to pigs when their time is up. So, the spider tries to think of different ways that the pig's life is worth sparing. She keeps trying to define what makes him special.

Despite that he is a pig, she sees greatness in him. The people in the surrounding towns come to see him and the amazing words that keep showing up in the spider's web. Then they leave because it's only interesting for a little while. The pig does not know how to define his own greatness. He is a humble little leader and so is the spider. Because of both of them, the animals start to see their worlds much more differently. No matter what the pig does with the spider's help, the farmer keeps seeing the pig as bacon and not as the greatest pig ever. The spider does not give up trying to differentiate her dear friend.

One of the last words the spider weaved in her web was "humble." She felt like this word perfectly described the pig. Interestingly, like many great leaders, he did not think that he was worthy of such a label. In this instant, the farmer and the crowds understood this pig's special significance. It didn't matter that he was not the fattest pig in town. He still won the best pig contest for the town, and his life was spared. He received the medal.

When the pig was awarded the medal, the farmer was asked to say some words. Here is what he said: In a time when we don't see many miraculous things or maybe we do and they are all around us, but don't know where to look, this is a true miracle.

The pig remained humble, and Charlotte continued weaving words she saw represented in the pig. She died after having many hundreds of baby spiders. With pig still alive and well, and new life in the air, the town felt different, as if they realized they lived someplace special. It made them act special too.

CONTRACT REINFORCEMENT

It is the manager's responsibility to find what makes each team member special and bring it to life whenever possible. Write down what makes each of your team members unique and great, and then make sure to share it with them.

EARN AND MAINTAIN THEIR TRUST

There's nothing greater in the world than when somebody on the team does something good, and everybody gathers around to pat him on the back.

BILLY MARTIN

I have heard the horror stories of managers taking credit for the work of their teams. Some managers feel threatened by ambitious and persistent team members. Instead of lifting their teams up, they may even shake them off one leg and keep them from moving up the career ladder for fear that they may try to "take their job." Managers who are not interested in being leaders and couldn't care less if their team members stay with them will consistently fail to recognize their team members' efforts and resort to taking credit where credit is absolutely not due.

I recall one of my managers who loved to gather insights and information from his direct reports, and then share the ideas with the executive team as if they were his own. I am assuming he lacked the originality to come up with his own innovative ideas, or maybe he wanted to be sure that no one else appeared smarter than he. Whatever his intentions, this type of management behavior led to increased distrust and doubt from his team members about whether he really cared about them and wanted to see them be successful.

If you are not a part of this type of shortsighted mindset and want to grow as a leader, it is most important that you recognize your team members' efforts and the results that they bring to the table. This includes recognition in front of the team, in one-on-one meetings, or maybe writing about them in the company newsletter.

Trust underlies the psychological contract in a fundamental way. This contract is not in writing. When team members accept a role with an organization, they need to trust that the organizational leaders will live up to their side of the bargain.

CASE IN POINT

A while back, I watched Million Dollar Arm, a great and inspiring
film about an almost-washed-up sports agent who has an idea to look
for talent in a foreign country and teach them to be baseball greats.
I must admit that I am not a big sports buff, but my husband and boys
are. So I decided to take this as family bonding time and watch it. I was
delightfully surprised to find a touching movie that was about baseball,
but was also about much more.

The agent set his sights on India as the place he would find cricket talent
that he hoped to mold into baseball greats. He was not prepared to find
the cluster of huts and people as he was destined to find. He was also not
prepared to see how many young men would gather to try to land their
chance at "greatness."

After many tryouts and traveling the country searching for the select
couple of future baseball legends, he found two young men. Although
they had never played baseball, they had very innate talents for throwing
the ball at fast speeds. Before traveling with the two men back home to
America to start their training, the agent went to the young men's village
and met their families and friends. I was struck by how he was impacted
by seeing that these two young men were so close with their families and
village people. This was not something he had seen before.

As he flew home with the young men, his eyes were set on getting
back on track and getting "back on top" as a sports agent. He would
soon find out that what he saw in that tiny village would be the ticket
to his true success.

After they arrived in America, it took some time for the young men
to become acclimated. I say this loosely as I am sure you can imagine
this would not be an easy feat. The agent had unreasonably high hopes
for the "future greats" and really did not grasp what it would take to
create a happy ending. As a result of long hours, minimal support, and
no family support, the young men became overwhelmed and lost their
way. The agent became increasingly frustrated as his future was on the
line. He took the boys as far as he could doing things "his way" and then
realized that he needed to be their family. They needed him to believe
in them and to treat them not as something to be owned or "made to be

successful," but as valued members of a team. They needed to be treated like individuals with unique needs. They needed to know that he would back them no matter what.

Once he began to put his needs aside and focus on the mental health of those young men and treat them as full partners in this exciting venture, the young men's performance soared! He gained their trust.

BUILD UPON THEIR STRENGTHS

When employees feel that their organization cares and encourages them to make the most of their strengths, they are more likely to respond with increased discretionary effort, a higher work ethic, and more enthusiasm and commitment.

In Gallup's March 9, 2015, update on engagement, it reiterated that only a third of U.S. employees are engaged at work, half (50.3%) are "not engaged," and 16.8% are "actively disengaged." One of the drivers here is that many organizations fail to focus on uncovering and then leveraging each employee's unique strengths.

Teams that focus on strengths every day have 12.5% greater productivity.
GALLUP 2014 - STATE OF THE AMERICAN WORKPLACE

Think about it.

If you could spend the majority of your time at work performing tasks that highlight your strengths, wouldn't you be happier?

In fact, for most of us, if we could spend most of our days focusing on our strengths, we would even work for free. (Okay, this might be a stretch, but you get my point.) Organizations that have discovered how to extract the natural talents and strengths of their employees are more productive, more profitable, and more adored.

CONTRACT REINFORCEMENT

When managers realize the power they have to impact employee happiness and engagement, they also realize that being a manager is no easy task. Organizations that provide leadership development opportunities and incentives to their managers to pay attention to the power they yield fare much better than those who fail to uncover this insight. Commit to that education.

EMPOWER THEM

We read a lot about the positive impacts of empowering employees to improve their work environment and the customer experience. Supporting this concept is not just another employee engagement tactic. It also gives power back to the employee to receive the true value from the work to which they commit and for which they long.

Many managers are afraid to relinquish control over their teams and the work that they do, because it may make them look bad, or even worse, make one of their team members look good! Temkin Group research points to the fact that engaged employees are 78% more likely to do something that is good for their company even if it is not expected of them. Temkin also uncovered that "companies with superior financial performance have 1.6 times as many engaged employees as do companies with lagging financial performance."

I recently had the opportunity to interview a couple of very strong and caring managers for a customer of mine. The habit that spoke to me the loudest was that they put their full trust in their team members to deliver a great customer experience to their customers.

Does it always happen? Not always, but it happens most of the time.

Do the managers coach and provide the required tools and direction for their teams to thrive?

Absolutely!

In the end, though, it was the managers' expectations and trust that their team members were just as committed as they were to being their best for the customer that made all of the difference.

We all want to have some ownership in the work that we do every day. This is a crucial component for long-term employee retention.

Once managers realize that empowering employees also increases their career dividends, they can truly begin to have a positive organizational impact.

CONTRACT REINFORCEMENT

What can you do to empower your team members to innovate on behalf of the organization and its customers? Meet with your team members and ask them what might be holding them back from being their best. Help them take back their personal power.

IT ALL STARTS WITH YOU

You can build a mansion with two hands but if you wanna build an empire you would need more hands. Every employer needs to respect and take care of those hands or else his dream of a successful business will just be a dream.

(READER COMMENT)

The concepts found within this Law are not rocket science. The overarching message is that managers are either the largest barriers to employee happiness or the most direct means to achieve it. When we take into consideration that the psychological contract exists between real people and not just corporate structures, we can see how the role of the manager is crucial when thinking about the Meeting of the Minds.

LAW #2

RECOGNIZE YOUR EMPLOYEES OFTEN

- 30% more of the workforce is satisfied when there's even an informal recognition program in place.

- 75% of employees receiving at least monthly recognition (even if informal) are satisfied with their job.

- 79% of employees who quit their jobs cite a lack of appreciation as a key reason for leaving.

While no one likes to fail, it is much more important for an employee to know that taking chances to do the right thing will be acknowledged, not punished. Nobody hits a home run every time. When people feel their contributions are unappreciated, they will stop trying.

MARK SANBORN, THE FRED FACTOR

Years ago, I worked in an organization that had a neat way of instilling the act of recognition in their culture. They created these cards that any employee could use to recognize another for just doing good work. They were black and white and very basic, but were accessible to everyone to use. I was impressed by how much people used them. The most impacting part was how much pride the recipients had when they received the cards. They would post them on their cubicle walls. It was a symbol of accomplishment and pride in the work that they did together every day.

As a member of the senior leadership team at this organization, I remember receiving 360 feedback from one of my colleagues that I focused too much on recognition. The comment was "No one has that much time to recognize people all of the time!" To be clear, I was not recognizing the same people non-stop. I just took the time to notice the little things that employees did to move the business forward and or exhibit great teamwork in the process.

Recognizing those around me is a priority for me. I also love to be recognized. I get it; not everyone is motivated by recognition, nor are they motivated to recognize the great works of others. Nonetheless, research shows that employees will not recall recognition if they are not recognized every seven days. I know that this sounds overwhelming, but managers must strive to provide it more frequently.

Why don't we recognize?

- "I'm afraid of jealousy if I recognize."
- "It's too easy to be inconsistent."
- "If I recognize too much, it will lose meaning."
- "We catch up with them at raise time."
- "They only want cash as a reward."
- "She/he already gets too much recognition."
- "I don't have time to recognize."
- "I don't want to play favorites."
- "My people don't care about or need recognition."

A while back I led a customer experience team for an organization that had a couple of ways to recognize their employees, but lacked more informal methods to show appreciation. I worked to institute a couple of additional informal ways to recognize employees. One of the recognition tools was a certificate program that we gave out once a year on Customer Experience Day.

I did not make the qualification for the certificate a difficult process, because I knew that in a large organization such as that one, only a few would get recognized and I considered it a success if the requirements were less stringent and more people received a certificate. I contacted the department heads to give me the names of those stars who stood out in their areas for providing great internal and or external customer service. Some were very reluctant to pick just a few among their larger department. One department head communicated that he could not choose any stars, because everyone on his team provided amazing service. I said to him, "Well, if that is true, then just give me all of their names and they all get a certificate!" Another department head argued the same thing and said that, because he did not want to cause animosity amongst the troops he would not recognize any of the team.

We must move past the "everyone gets a ribbon" mentality and recognize our rock stars frequently or else we risk losing the bunch. All employees like recognition. Based upon their personality and communication style, they may want to be recognized differently. Nonetheless, we would be hard-pressed to find an employee who does not want to feel good about the work that they do.

THE CART BEFORE THE HORSE

Which comes first, a motivated employee or the recognition of the employee for the work they do? I would argue that a leader must first know what motivates each of their team members before he/she can set out to recognize them. This is because not all forms of recognition are effective for or desired by every person.

Have you ever seen the very quiet team member cower when recognized in front of a large group? Have you noticed that outgoing person who runs in all directions to seek out public recognition?

According to famed psychologist David McClelland, there are three basic types of motivation: 1) Achievement, 2) Authority and 3) Affiliation.

Achievement Seekers

Those who seek Achievement are looking for the following things:
- They attain realistic but challenging goals.
- Achieving the task is its own reward.
- Financial reward is a measurement of success.
- Security/status are not the primary motivators.
- Feedback is a quantifiable measure of success.
- They seek improvement.

Authority Seekers

Employees who seek Authority are looking for the following things:
- They value their ideas being heard and prevailing.
- Having influence and impact is the most important reward.
- They show leadership skills and enjoy directing others.
- Increasing personal status and prestige is important.

Affiliation Seekers

Employees who are motivated by Affiliation are looking for the following things:

- They need friendly relationships and are motivated by interaction with others.
- Being liked and held in high regard is important.
- They are team players.
- Emotions are a larger motivating factor than quantifiable data.
- They are in tune with others' feelings and seek to make others happy.

What motivates you?

WAYS TO RECOGNIZE BASED UPON MOTIVATION

The simple but transformative act of a leader expressing appreciation to a person in a meaningful and memorable way is the missing accelerator that can do so much and yet is used so sparingly.

ADRIAN GOSTICK AND CHESTER ELTON, THE CARROT PRINCIPLE

Organizations need to build systems that create environments for consistent recognition. There is no need for balloons and parties all the time. They want to feel valued for their work, and to take pride in the work that they do.

Find out what floats their boat. Ask them. Get to know them.

In line with Mr. McClelland's motivation theory:

Achievement Seekers will prefer to be recognized one-on-one or in a team meeting. You need to be specific about what they achieved. Even better, point to how what they did helped the team or the organization accomplish goals. This group would gather even more motivation if their achievement was compared to others on a leaderboard. Finally, if you are able to tie a bonus to this achievement, the Accomplishment-seeking employee will feel appreciated.

Authority Seekers feel that they are successful when they are promoted into higher positions of authority. These employees will feel accomplished when they have more control and responsibility throughout their day. Look to set a clear and definite career path for this group. Let them take on special projects that have significant exposure.

Affiliation Seekers long for positive relationships with others. They would not want to be limited in their ability to connect with and touch other lives. If you want to recognize this group, allowing them to lead committees of coworkers in common goals would be the best way to do that. For the introvert in this group, providing them opportunities to take part in groups of employees would be a big perk. They would also feel good about themselves if they are selected to mentor others.

CONTRACT REINFORCEMENT

Don't use the same old way to recognize everyone on your team. Take the time to find out what will make them feel appreciated. Use these options to help you customize their recognition and praise.

LET'S CROWDSOURCE IT!

In a 2016 study, Gallup looked at employee recognition and found that the most memorable recognition comes most often from an employee's manager (28 percent), followed by a high-level leader or CEO (24 percent), the manager's manager (12 percent), a customer (10 percent) and peers (9 percent).

The study also recommended that employees receive some form of formal recognition every seven days. However, given the time formal recognition requires and leaders' increasing workloads, this suggestion appears unreasonable.

One way to solve this problem is to crowdsource recognition.

When I refer to crowdsourcing recognition, I mean that organizations should plan to include and embrace a multi-tiered approach to recognize employees. By planning and opening up the recognition pipeline, organizations take the pressure off managers to do all of the heavy lifting. While an employee's manager is still the most important recognition source from whom employees should receive recognition, hearing praise from others outside of that employee-manager relationship can be the difference between an employee feeling valued or not feeling valued at all.

Below is an illustration of a crowd-sourced recognition structure.

Figure A *illustrates suggested structure to set up for recognition.*

Organizational Recognition

Organizational recognition would take the form of birthdays, anniversaries, service awards and "Employee of the Month"-like celebrations. This level of recognition tends to be less frequent and more formal. Because there are many employees, not everyone can receive this type of recognition.

It leaves many out, but does serve its purpose. Instituting these forms of recognition begins to bond your employees with your brand. Nonetheless, it does not fully serve the employees' needs of being recognized more often, and the responsibility to see this level of recognition to successful implementation rests in the hands of human resources. HR cannot and should not be the keeper of the recognition flame. We need to look at the next level: recognition by a manager.

Manager Recognition

This level of recognition is by far the most influential and long-lasting for employees. In most cases, the manager hired the employee whom they are now managing. The employee likes to know that the manager still perceives that the employee is adding value in accordance with the original psychological contract that the parties entered early on in the relationship.

This type of recognition might take the form of a simple "thank you for all you do" in a one-on-one meeting. At a team meeting, the manager might even say, "Jessica did a great job improving this process. Nice work, Jessica!" It can be more formal with a point system for different types of positive behaviors that allow employees to buy movie tickets or dinner out with their significant other. A thank-you note would be just fine too.

The point is that the formality of recognition is not as important at this level as the frequency of the recognition. An employee's relationship with their manager is crucial to their overall experience with the employer's brand. However, depending upon the size of a manager's team, it can be very difficult to quench the thirst of the employee who thrives on recognition as a part of their job. This is where the idea of crowdsourcing recognition really gains momentum.

Coworker recognition

Over the years, I have found that coworker recognition is a great way to fill the potential gaps that exist in the first two levels of recognition. What processes do you have in place to help all coworkers recognize when they see the good deeds of others?

TINYpulse, an employee feedback, recognition, and performance management software company, created Cheers for Peers, a coworker recognition module. Ketti Salemme, the company's former senior communications manager, told me that they "realized that managers don't see all the things employees do. When other employees send recognition, it goes miles. The cool thing is that managers can see what others are seeing and can mention it so that their work does not go unnoticed."

Salemme also said the company streams Cheers for Peers recognition on a big screen TV, so that the CEO or anyone who walks through the door can see what the team is up to. Then, others can give kudos after they see this. This also allows others in different departments to see what is happening.

Customer Recognition

Finally, customers can also help to recognize employees. There are organizations that have formalized this by offering short "happy face" transactional surveys that are either emailed to customers immediately following an interaction or that are in the employee's signature line. I have even used positive survey feedback at weekly team meetings to reinforce customer service excellence. There is often gold in the verbatim survey comments.

A LITTLE GOES A LONG WAY

It's easy to get caught up in day-to-day affairs, and forget to stop and take a minute to praise employees who are doing great work.

Recently, one of my clients told me that she works hard to recognize her direct reports and colleagues, because she used to have a very demeaning boss who only talked down to her. He just never had a positive thing to say to my client. He would not even say "thank you."

After staying with that organization for as long she could, she left, and was blessed enough to land the leadership position she has now. She admits that recognition never used to be all that important to her until she had a boss who didn't believe in it.

Did I mention that she took a $15,000 a year pay cut to make this move?

This is the truth. Many employees are not looking for big trophies;

they just want more recognition for the work that they do. In a 2013 survey, Glassdoor uncovered that four in five (81 percent) employees say they're motivated to work harder when their boss shows appreciation for their work.

Recognizing employees when they do great work will go a long way in empowering employees.

Managers who clear away the fray from their daily tasks to take time to notice their team's efforts to improve customer experience will receive great dividends. Don't complicate it. Just say thank you and how much you appreciate their contribution to improving your customers' experience.

By considering the many ways to recognize the efforts of employees and allowing such praise to come from different sources, organizations can then comply with psychological contract principles. An employee's most basic expectation from an employer is that they will feel valued for the work that they do for the organization.

TINYpulse's 2015 Employee Engagement Report found that when asking whether employees feel valued at work, only 26% strongly agreed. This is concerning, since the number dropped by 16% from the previous year.

CONTRACT REINFORCEMENT

If you are a manager, how often do you recognize your team members? Remember, know how your team member likes to receive recognition. Some don't like big parties and balloons. Many just prefer a "thank you." Be sure to use their name and be as specific as possible about the reason for the recognition. This way, they know what types of behaviors drive positive praise from you.

LAW #3

GIVE THEM A VOICE AND DO

SOMETHING ABOUT IT

How do you expect your employees to be in alignment with company goals, if you don't let them know how they impact the bottom line? Employees who feel valued are eager to contribute to the success of their companies. Don't assume that they know this. Keep the doors of communication open and remind them that their feedback is important.

(READER COMMENT)

Employees feel valued and successful when they feel their voice is heard. Not only that, they feel like a vested member of the organizations when, at least, some of their voice leads to positive change.

Organizations that master the full communication/action loop related to employee feedback keep them engaged and excited about the work that they do. They begin to feel more powerful. That feeling of power will keep them bonded to you longer.

WHAT IS YOUR EMPLOYEE LISTENING STRATEGY?

To be listened to is, generally speaking, a nearly unique experience for most people. It is enormously stimulating. It is small wonder that people who have been demanding all their lives to be heard so often fall speechless when confronted with one who gravely agrees to lend an ear. Man clamors for the freedom to express himself and for knowing that he counts. But once offered these conditions, he becomes frightened.

ROBERT C. MURPHY

Believe it or not, your organization needs an employee listening strategy.

What do I mean by this?

Many organizations administer an annual employee engagement survey and then stop there. By doing just that, they miss the opportunity to truly listen to what their employees like or dislike about the organization, their manager, their role, and more.

This also undermines the most valuable reason for listening: Action!

Here are some things to consider when crafting an employee listening strategy:

Why Are You Listening?

For organizations that administer employee engagement surveys annually, they often do not know why they are doing it. Is it just to say that your employees have a voice? Is it to tell employees that you "listen" to them frequently?

Why are you listening?

Is your employees' happiness and satisfaction the end, or is there an underlying reason your organization wants to ask your employees questions annually?

Knowing the "why" behind any employee listening program is crucial, because then everything else can fall in line.

> *One of the most sincere forms of respect is actually listening to what another has to say.*
>
> BRYANT H. MCGILL

The Importance

Every single one of us longs to be heard. It is innate. Think about a baby who wants to get the attention of the adults in her life. What does she do? Makes a lot of adorable and funny sounds to make her presence known. How does she feel valued and important? She sees how those same adults respond to what they hear. When they hop into action to meet her needs, she knows that her sounds mean something to those around her. Her voice is power.

If You Do Nothing

If the adults sat there and did nothing, what do you think might happen? Would the baby become silent? Perhaps, if she made enough sounds and no one ever responded.

Would she scream and throw things? Perhaps, if she felt like there was no other way to get their attention.

I know it may seem odd that I am comparing a baby to an employee, but the point is that we all want to believe that our voices mean something to others. We want to know that the sounds that come from our mouths will resonate with those who hear us. That when we divulge our concerns, thoughts, anger, and desires in focus groups, surveys, or other feedback mechanisms, positive change will come about.

By soliciting the Voice of the Employee, are organizations committing to changing everything?

Absolutely not!

WHAT DOES IT MEAN TO COMMIT?

Just because organizational leadership solicits employee feedback, does not mean that the organization commits to act on every piece of the Voice of the Employee. Having said that, there are some very clear steps to take when receiving the feedback to foster the feeling of being valued and important:

Take It All In

After you have gathered all of the feedback, take some time to understand what it is saying to and about your organization. Look for trends and outliers in the comments. Take it all in and process it. Categorize it to make sure you get the full story.

Plan Of Attack

After you have taken the time to understand the feedback, it is critical that senior leaders and business unit heads come together to decide which items to conquer. Using the trends in the data to set strategic priorities will be the difference between having a true Voice of the Employee program and just asking a lot of questions. Getting the buy-in and assigning accountability for the results is an important step.

Report Out

Once your organizational leaders have had time to take in the feedback and come up with a plan for what to do about what they heard, it is time to report out what was heard and explain the next steps to the entire organization.

I do not mean that every little comment and fact should be reported to all employees. To the contrary, the report out should be very high level, restating only big themes and then the top few actions that the leaders plan to take based upon the feedback. This is crucial, because this is when employees begin to see that the time they spent providing feedback was not in vain.

Put Action To It

Now that you have disclosed the big themes and said what you will do, you must go about doing what you said you would do. Even more important, involve employees at all levels in the organization in the change that they are seeking. Create employee councils. Help them to help you bring the Voice of the Employee to life. It is the action that makes giving the feedback worthwhile!

Connect the dots

You have put in a lot of work taking in the feedback, planning what to do about it, letting them know what you heard, and putting action to key elements of the feedback. Now it's just as important to make sure that you continually communicate how your efforts are improving their experience.

Use different modes of communication and make sure to clearly connect the dots between the big themes you heard and the actions you are taking in response to the themes. Make sure to visually show that the entire organization is getting behind the changes. Use storytelling to help them understand how important their voices are.

CONTRACT REINFORCEMENT

It is crucial that organizational leaders not take their employees' voices for granted. You do not need to change every area related to their feedback for them to feel heard. Let them know that you are asking because you want to know the truth and are prepared to put in effort to improve their experience. Otherwise, you may notice that they, like the little baby, may fall silent with apathy, or cause a ruckus with negative energy. Worse yet, they may walk out the door without ever giving you a chance to create your best culture yet!

HOW WILL YOU LISTEN?

There are myriad ways to gather the "voice" of your employees, the most popular of which is the annual survey. While annual surveys are great for organizational benchmarking and gauging your employees' overall relationship with your organization, there are many ways to get unfiltered and trustworthy feedback from your employees.

Pulse Surveys

Pulse surveys are real-time surveys that are short and provide immediate feedback to managers and the organization. They are excellent tools to drive more employee engagement and create a culture of transparency. Platforms like, TINYpulse, help organizations gather this anonymous feedback by asking just one question per week to gauge employee engagement and provide actionable insights.

Managers Meetings

Whether we are talking about team meetings or one-on-one meetings, managers have a unique opportunity to clear away the barriers to true employee listening. These meetings should remain the safe place for parties to ask questions and provide feedback. When managers listen to their team members, it promotes trust and honesty. This is the perfect combination for a successful relationship.

All Employee Meetings

I do not believe that "all-hands" employee meetings are the more credible way to gather a big picture of employee sentiment. Nonetheless, it is a great way to share information and get an initial pulse of opinion. I like to call this the "allergic reaction" that the information sharing may create. Once you gauge that initial response, you can plan for more pointed feedback methods to follow.

Focus Groups

I really enjoy and am quite successful gathering unfiltered feedback via focus groups. I usually recommend a good cross-section of employees. I do not include supervisors in these groups unless I am meeting with that group, because I find that employees cannot loosen up and open-up with management present.

One-On-One Interviews

This is one of the most effective ways to gather raw feedback, particularly if they trust the interviewer and know that their feedback will remain anonymous. This is where the rubber meets the road with employee listening, because I have found that employees rarely hold back.

Employee Happiness Audits

In many cases, human resources or some other internal resource may be the ones gathering this feedback. Unfortunately, more often than not, employees don't trust those internal stakeholders for a variety of reasons. In this case, it may make sense to bring in an outside consultant to use some of the methods above to gather unfiltered feedback. This may seem counter-intuitive to some, but often the outside consultant is perceived as non-affiliated or non-interested, and thus, automatically garners more trust. You will know what will work for your organization when the time arrives.

Stay Interviews

There is a growing trend toward conducting employee-stay interviews in place of, or in addition to, exit interviews. This is primarily due to unsuccessful attempts to gather trustworthy feedback from people on their way out the door. It turns out that current employees are much more likely to give human resources the time of day and even sit to talk about the work environment. Also, they are more likely to provide balanced feedback.

WHAT WILL YOU DO AFTER YOU HAVE LISTENED?

So, what will you do with the feedback once you gather it?

What is your plan of action?

One key reason you are asking the questions you are asking is so you can respond to your employees' specific needs and suggestions.

The absolute worst thing you could do is to gather feedback and then just sit on it and do or say nothing at all about it again. This will be the fastest way to break down trust between the organization and the people who keep it moving forward.

You may also never "hear" from them again.

Here are a few things to consider in this regard.

Who Decides What Gets Fixed?

Have you established some type of governing body that can review the feedback or employee suggestions and decide what gets fixed or acted upon? Please do not keep all of the feedback housed with the senior leadership team and expect that they will have time to make needed improvements.

Should they be a part of the deciding team? Yes, but there are other key influencers who should be a part of the process as well.

Who Is Accountable To Act?

Once you have decided who will be a part of the reviewing body, you will also need to know who is responsible to act on the feedback.

Would it be beneficial to have the leaders directly responsible for the area or teams providing the specific feedback to be the ones to lead the improvement efforts? Alternatively, should you appoint non-interested persons to lead the improvement efforts? These questions and more are things to consider when considering who is accountable to follow through on the feedback.

How Do You Track Improvements?

This can be easy or this can be hard. Much of the difference rests on the internal tools that are available to "close the loop" and track efforts that are taken to act on the feedback.

No matter what tools are available, someone has to facilitate the creation of action plans and measure the success of improvement efforts in the organization. If you leave this part of the listening strategy to chance, you might as well never ask the question. It is in acting upon the listening that trust is built and culture is curated.

Remember, in the end, it is just as important to act on feedback as it is to listen or ask to hear your employees' voices. Organizations that do both will make employees feel valued and heard. Who wouldn't want to stay at a place that produces that result?

WHAT IS THERE TO BE AFRAID ABOUT?

You gain strength, courage, and confidence by every experience in which you really stop to look fear in the face. You must do the thing which you think you cannot do.

ELEANOR ROOSEVELT

Do you ever notice how we often shy away from things we have never tried before? Even if we have tried something previously and did not see immediate results, we often feel uncomfortable trying it again.

This is what often happens in the business world. Everyone is busy starting and completing projects, setting visions, and executing them. So, what's missing?

The employees' input into it all.

Many businesses make assumptions about what their employees want and need without first involving them in the decision-making process. In the end, you know what they say about assumptions. If we steer clear of making them, our business might reflect what the employee really wants. There are three main reasons why organizational leaders fail to ask and then act upon employee feedback:

They really don't want to know

You know the cliché, "What you don't know won't hurt you."

Many companies are fine walking the road that they pave without their employees' input. In fact, some even feel like frontline employees bring no value to the conversation, and that they know what is best. This is, of course, the wrong way to do business and potentially deadly to any company looking to grow and retain great talent.

I would suggest an alternative way of looking at things. If the strategy that you are trying to employ is that good, test it out with employees before pushing forward. Let them sniff-test it first. Believe me, not knowing is not equal to employee-centric.

They lack clear direction and process

Many companies long to be the next Zappos but lack the clear direction and process to inspire such focus.

Many companies know that if they collect employee feedback, they must do something about it. These same companies just do not understand that building long-term mutually beneficial relationships with employees is mostly about putting sustainable processes in place.

This includes processes for receiving and responding to feedback, in earnest. For companies that do it well, this means establishing a closed-loop process wherein everyone knows who will follow up and when.

In the end, clear direction from leadership and consistency in the follow-up process are key elements of a robust employee feedback program.

They don't have the resources to own the next steps

Sometimes, it is not that companies do not want to hear from their employees or even that they lack a process. Often, companies simply do not have the needed staff to respond to feedback. This is especially true in smaller companies that may lack capital to expand to include more post-sale customer-focused team members.

Many companies continue to pour money into sales teams without thinking through the ramifications of feedback that is never received or never acted upon.

There may be a need to shift thinking to "how do we make sure to keep all of the customers our awesome sales folks are bringing through the door?"

Employees who are fanatical about an organization's brand don't just come from thin air. They are developed over time.

WRAPPING IT UP

Organizations that focus on using the voices of their employees to drive improvements and innovation will always end up on top. Although feeling like they are heard feels good to employees, organizations must understand that it is the process behind the scenes that creates the positive feelings. This Law is connected to the psychological contract most directly, because organization's that successfully execute a listening strategy can clearly articulate and understand employee wants and needs. This level of understanding helps them fulfill their end of the deal.

CONTRACT REINFORCEMENT

Take time to map out your listening process. Better yet, map out your employees' complete experience and then use the feedback you receive from your listening program to smooth out the gaps in their journey. Taking the time to do this will speak volumes and produce wonderful retention results.

LAW #4

GROW AND PROMOTE THEIR TALENTS

78% said they would remain longer with their employer
if they saw a career path with the current organization.

According to TINYpulse's 2017 Employee Engagement Report, titled
The Broken Bridges of the Workplace, professional development ranked
third as a driver for employee happiness. In this report, TINYpulse found
that only 26% of employees feel there are adequate opportunities for
professional growth. When asked if employees felt that their promotion
and career path was clear to them, only 49% believe so.

There are so many hidden gems within your workforce. Organizations
that fail to put a process in place to find those gems will lose the talent
acquisition and retention race.

CASE IN POINT

As embarrassing as this may sound, many years ago, after moving into
my current home I discovered that I have a plum tree right in my front
yard. One of my next-door neighbors who was about to move out of his
home confessed that he picked up plums that would fall in his yard and
mine for the couple of years he lived there.

I sat baffled as he told me the stories of all of the delicious jams and
breads he made from the juicy plums that fell from my tree. I questioned
whether he was joking and how I never saw one plum in my yard, we
have seen very few plums on our tree.

I even confirmed what a plum tree looks like by looking on Google.

It was, in fact, a plum tree!

I live in Colorado where the weather is hit-or-miss with hail and snow
and heat and bugs that eat at the leaves of trees. Regretfully, since finding
out that we do have a large plum tree in my front yard, we have not seen
one plum grow on our tree.

Some may ask how the heck we didn't know or how we missed that
plums were growing on our tree.

Here is my answer: I do not have a green thumb. I have a busy life with children and career. Many days, I came in my garage and closed it only to wake up to do the same thing the next day.

I was not very good at smelling the roses, or in this case, outside long enough to notice the juicy plums in our tree.

After that conversation with that long-gone neighbor, that has changed. Now, I keep looking at the tree hoping that a plum will show up. I am going to commit to pruning the tree on a schedule and feeding it with great nutrients.

This life lesson parallels what happens with organizations that fail to take a good look at the potential future leaders in their organizations. Those high-potential employees fail to thrive, because they were never nourished, or never chosen to display how ripe they were for growth.

When was the last time your organization conducted a firm review of the "plums" that are sitting in your offices, or out in the field?

Here are a few ways to ensure that your organization doesn't make the mistake I made by failing to leverage the strengths and potential of current employees.

SUCCESSION PLANNING IS KEY

Growing other leaders from the ranks isn't just the duty of the leader, it's an obligation.

WARREN BENNIS

Much has been written on succession planning. It is an important point. Many organizations think that they have done all they can to protect against key employee losses, but have they really nourished the fruit inside their own organizations?

Planning for future losses must be more than a conversation. A detailed plan with tactical steps must be put in place before leaders can rest on their laurels.

It has been my experience that there are plenty of gifted and passionate people inside of many organizations, but for a variety of reasons, they are passed over for promotion or for development opportunities.

The key here is to consider the whole person when deciding whom to develop and to train to higher levels of the organization.

Just as Warren Bennis said in this section's opening quote, it is the obligation of any organization to develop its people. Any worthwhile succession plan must bear fruit for internal employees who are prepared to go the distance. This is a crucial element of the psychological contract. Whether spoken or unspoken, employees expect to grow while working for the organizations from which they accept offers.

LEVERAGE ALL VOICES

I have a novel thought: What if organizations included frontline employees in the succession-planning discussions?

They are the ones whose leaders will eventually leave the organization. Those same employees know what a good leader is made of just as they are painfully aware of what highly underdeveloped leaders act like.

Why won't senior teams consider expanding the groups or individuals who have a say in the process? Think about it: Line staff often help "prune" the leaders' rough edges by teaching them what it means to lead.

Wouldn't it make sense to formally include their voices? Giving the frontline a little more credit for what they know about the great leaders who may exist in the current lineup will go a long way toward empowering them.

TRAIN UP

> *Survival of the fittest is not the same as survival of the best.*
> *Leaving leadership development up to chance is foolish.*
> **MORGAN MCCALL**

I love this quote by Morgan McCall! It makes me think of how making uninformed assumptions about people and circumstances is always a bad idea.

What I love most about developing and training high-potential employees is that it works to retain them longer while also building a stronger bench for the organization.

Many leaders look at developing their people the wrong way. Some are afraid that they may look bad when others are growing and developing. I think most would agree that this type of leader is not a leader after all.

Anyone who seeks to appear more important by diminishing the potential in others can never be a leader. Organizations that create leadership development opportunities for high-potential employees and also create access to projects or roles that stretch these same people are the ones that will be more successful in succession-planning efforts.

Don't just sit by and let perfectly talented employees walk out your door because you failed to harvest the potential within them.

In a 2015 report, TINYpulse uncovered the top three reasons employees don't have professional growth opportunities:

1. Feel too siloed and/or not given new projects
2. No open discussion of career opportunities
3. Have background/skills not being used

These are compelling insights for any organization to consider and eradicate if the goal is long-term retention rates.

Personally, I always strived to grow my team members. I wanted the best for them inside and outside of work. This usually entailed frequent conversations about short-term and long-term goals. As a manager, I needed to find out what made my team members excited, where they saw themselves, and how I, as a manager in the organization, could facilitate their goal attainment.

Organizations that have low employee engagement lack the structure to develop their most valuable asset: their people.

Then there are those organizations like Zappos, Google, and LinkedIn, to name a few, that have discovered the hidden gems in their own workforce when they continue to train and develop their employees to become their very best. By doing so, they demonstrate that they care about each employee – not just for what that development can do for their organizations, but also for what that development means to the employees personally.

BE OPEN ABOUT THE PATH

In TINYpulse's 2017 report, they uncovered that only 25% of employees feel management is transparent about career progression opportunities.

In that report, they provided some quotes of direct employee feedback on this topic:

- "I'm not quite sure what promotions, if any, are or are not available to me or my colleagues at our level. There seems to be a high rateof turnover that may be, in part, due to a lack of clarity on how to grow within the business."

- "While I feel like there is a lot of future opportunity in the organization, I have no idea how to get promoted. My manager has never discussed development or promotion opportunities with me."

- "It has never been explained to me what each role entails and what I need to achieve in order to progress. I have only been told by my current and past team leader to 'carry on how you're doing,' which is a compliment. However, it would be better if everyone was given some sort of document which consists of targets you need to hit in order to progress in the company."

What I find most compelling about these employee thoughts is that they appear to want to make their psychological contract work with their employer. They are all but begging to help move the organization forward by using their gifts. They are simply seeking clarity and opportunity.

INTERVIEW WITH A TALENT DEVELOPMENT EXPERT

I had the great luck to meet up with a talent development leader at Zappos. Rich Hazeltine was kind enough to give me his thoughts on talent development and talent mobility. I have reprinted that interview here, because the content is so relevant to this Law.

ME: "What role do you feel training and development play in creating engaged and loyal employees?"

RICHARD HAZELTINE: "I think it has a lot to do with setting expectations with folks just starting with you and with those leaders who need to maintain that energy. If entry-level folks understand what their horizon looks like and the leaders understand that they are the levers to everything, it can be impactful. As far as customer service goes, the leader understands that he/she has power to get employees going. The leader understands the he/she needs to remove barriers. As we move towards self-organization, the balance is in deciding how do you lead without managing. It is then more about managing your own performance ... hands off."

ME: "It sounds interesting, but it must be challenging to reverse what you know as the traditional model of management, right?"

HAZELTINE: "Well, I agree and not. If a leader has a high degree of emotional intelligence and is aware of their people and knows how to unlock what is great in their people, then it's not as hard. I have to say that I have changed my views on this in the last five to ten years. Good leaders are not micro-managing their teams. They are just unleashing them."

ME: "How does this differ for Millennials and then those over 35 years old?"

HAZELTINE: "Someone who is closer to my age group, it is harder. You know – someone who has been in the workplace longer is used to a more traditional setup. Younger employees can learn about it and not be clouded about their previous experience. In our model, there are those who want someone to give them problems to solve and fix instead of doing so much self-organization. That's part of the reason we had our recent losses as reported in The New York Times. Self-organization is tough and not many organizations have done it successfully. It's really hard to knock down walls to make it work."

ME: "What are your thoughts on the idea of employers facilitating talent mobility within the organization?"

HAZELTINE: "Zappos is a poster child on this. A good friend who works here came up to me with an interest in a particular area. I saw an internal job posting that I thought would be a great fit for her. I sent her the job posting, and just explained to her that I was not kicking her off the team, but I thought she should pursue it. She ended up taking that on and enjoying the new responsibility."

"If people are working on what they are passionate about, their work should be pretty good or they are certainly not going to put extra work in. We tend to have a pretty quick turnover in our Customer Loyalty Team (CLT), usually about three-six months. This is the team that handles customer contact via phone, email, and chat. Then they move around or outside of the CLT organization and managers are very happy to see them move on and into another part of the business. We have some who have moved from design to marketing or finance."

"There is a ton of mobility. The sky is the limit and really is about the way you pitch yourself. We have an internship-type program and then they are able to work maybe five hours in that area per week. If the business needs allow the internship in the other department, then employees are given the freedom to do it. Folks in the hourly ranks, especially even in CLT, get the opportunity to do that. It's kind of like a "try it before you buy it" program. Someone who was a part of the CLT took some classes and then became a project manager. Because of our new model, a person might hold five different roles and may not do work on those teams all the time, but have an anchor role. The leader decides who goes on what team and if they have time. It is a very fluid environment."

ME: "In the places you have worked, do you see a connection between helping employees learn and grow to their then delivering an excellent customer experience?"

HAZELTINE: "We talk about the Zappos family. It rolls over to the customers. Employees don't have to act differently with peers and leaders, and they can treat customers the same way. They don't have to smile to a crappy manager and then smile to the customer. I worked in restaurants and focused on making the environment right for the employees. If employees are treated fairly by their manager and people going over and above internally to point out the positive, then that translates over to customers. We don't believe in forcing people to act a different way."

My time with Rich was fruitful. I learned a lot, and he confirmed for me what I think many of us know, but do not always exercise: Organizations can create employees fanatical about their brands if they focus more time and resources on developing their leaders.

I particularly found Rich's decision to assess emotional intelligence and use insights to coach employees on their own data to be enlightening. This is empowerment!

THE MILLENNIAL FACTOR

> *75% of younger employees say lack of growth*
> *would lead them to look for a new job.*

I would be remiss if I did not address the "Millennial factor." I am speaking about it so formally, because this topic has been front and center in recent years. I have also been smack dab in the middle of "negative talk" about this special group of employees. The question becomes how "special" are they? The other thing to note is that this is not necessarily a homogeneous group. Just because we talk about them in that manner doesn't make it so.

I have placed this topic under this Law, because Millennials are most interested in organizations that focus on growing and promoting their talents. They often want many of the same things all other generations want, but it is their desire to constantly learn, grow, move forward, quickly, that sets them apart.

There are a few areas to consider when crafting a strategy to engage and retain the Millennials in your workforce:

Career Path

Millennials thrive on options. It's not as much about where they start, but where they have the potential to go and how fast. Organizations that include very clear career paths with timelines and triggers for promotion will keep this group of ambitious employees engaged for much longer periods of time.

Ability To Lead

I have witnessed it firsthand. I am sitting in a cross-functional meeting, and we are doing the usual tennis match of discussing next steps. Then, a Millennial employee interrupts with a very direct and astute solution. We are all then left sitting there wondering why we did not think of the brilliance.

Many Millennials are natural leaders. They are not debilitated by fear; instead, they are energized by the many possibilities. Some around the table are afraid of their confidence. I am impressed by it.

Focus On Innovation

I worked with a group of employees made up of many generations to drive a service culture. Our focus was on recognizing employees, listening to them, and highlighting great stories of internal and external service. We decided that we wanted to put together a large employee networking event that would allow them to connect with one another and minimize silos. It would also allow them to see what other positions were open to them in their careers.

At the same time, a group of Millennial employees was working on something very similar, but with some innovative twists to our concept. In short, we decided to work with one another to move toward the same goal.

During our first meeting, I recalled for them an interaction I had with mid-level managers when I first presented the idea. I could tell that the Millennial group was not very interested in hearing about the obstacles. They were committed to making their event happen. They wanted to innovate to make their experience in the workplace interesting. What I did not know is that they had already received preliminary approval from the highest level of the organization. My hint of any potential barriers was inconsequential. This was moving forward. One of that group said, "I am not concerned about approval, since so and so already gave us the go-ahead." They were committed to innovation and were prepared to remove any obstacle that stood in their way. "No" was not really an option.

Promote Connections

Working with that very talented and intelligent group of Millennials, I noticed how strongly they felt about connecting outside of work. They place great value in connections with others. They were not as much concerned with all of the formalities in the event, but in creating spaces and time to connect with their co-workers at a deeper level. I was pleasantly surprised by this insight, given the fact that many others complain that Millennials only care about texting and about themselves. I found the opposite to be true.

CONTRACT REINFORCEMENT

Don't just train to train. Make sure that your offerings align with core values and your mission. Make sure your training and development offerings tell a compelling story that aligns with what you want from your future leaders. Be a revolutionary, which then will allow your organization to inspire employees empowered to make smart decisions for the organization and its customers. Don't close your mind to the power of diverse thinking!

BE CREATIVE

Organizations that focus on being open to new ways to engage employees and leverage their strengths are successful. Here are a few ways to be creative in the area:

Mentor Programs

Employees of all ages enjoy learning from others. Mentoring programs provide rich soil for learning. Invest in a program that matches more seasoned leaders with newer employees to provide an additional means of growth and learning. It could even be open to any employees, no matter tenure, who simply want to move to a different place in their career. I mentored someone who was with the organization for a while, but she felt stuck in her current role. She also felt limited in her ability to move up or around. Together, we investigated her skills and things that energized her.

We took those insights to start to formulate a go-forward strategy for her career. It was a great process, I learned a lot from her as well.

Job-Shadowing

Why let employees go if you can keep their interest longer by allowing them to peek at the other side? Job shadowing is the method to allow this. This means that you set up the environment where employees can visit other departments and see what they do. It provides a clearer view for the employee who wants more than what they are currently experiencing.

Some organizations might see job shadowing as a threat to a stable work environment, because employees might become more focused on a move. I would challenge organizational leaders to think differently. What is more important: that you keep the employee in one particular job function or department, or keep the employee as an employee altogether? Choose to be creative with ways to keep your employees interested.

Talent Mobility

Consistent with the idea of job shadowing is the idea of talent mobility. Talent mobility simply means that you put the right people in the right places when they are needed based upon opportunities and unique skill sets. As described in my interview with the Zappos talent development leader, they formalized this process by layering the job shadowing idea with the basic retention strategy of allowing employees to transfer to different roles.

This is a key employee loyalty strategy and is in close alignment with the precepts of the psychological contract in that employers demonstrate that they are in tune with the employees' evolving expectations. Over time, employees are motivated by and attracted to different elements of the employment relationship. What got them there will not necessarily keep them loyal for long periods. Organizations that master the balance between job stability and job flexibility will retain top talent for much longer.

BE THE FLAME

*Treat people as if they were what they ought to be and you
help them to become what they are capable being.*

JOHANN WOLFGANG VON GOETHE

The best leaders see beyond what people currently are to what they have
the potential to be. Training and development continues to top the list
for U.S. employee engagement surveys. Yet, those same development
budgets are shrinking. There are many employees who stay with an
organization, because they are challenged with new roles and new
knowledge. Many leave for the opposite reason. I like to say that when
it comes to employee experience, love is in the details.

One of the best ways to empower frontline employees is to show
them their importance, by investing in their skills. The more skills
andconfidence they have, the more value they can add to the
organization.

CONTRACT REINFORCEMENT

Be a retention-innovator. Don't rely on doing what you have always done
to retain the best people you have. Be creative like the many organizations
who embrace flexible work arrangements. Investigate talent-mobility
options for interested employees. Lead outside the lines.

LAW #5

FOSTER DEEP

CONNECTIONS WITH THEM

Organizationally, connectedness means that the frontline looks to leadership to create a culture that speaks to them. They want to know that there is a plan for their safety, security, and future. Employees want to know that their managers and organizational leaders care. They do not want to feel like a number. They want to feel like the work that they do every day matters to customers, to their managers, and to the entire organization. It is this longing for connectedness that pushes employees to move from workplace to workplace.

CONNECTION TO MISSION AND VISION

Only 1 in 150 employees who says their organization does not have a set of values is fully engaged. One of the biggest failures that managers make is to expect great things from their team members without first setting a compelling vision for them to follow.

I recently read a *Forbes* article that reviewed the "Top 5 Reasons Employees Quit in 2013." Surprising to me was that many team members decided to move to another company when that company had a clear plan and appeared to be stable. This outranked the driver of increased compensation. It appears that the fad of candidates knocking down the doors of startups that exude innovation may be fading away.

No matter what type of organization you represent, the key to keeping team members engaged is being clear about where you are going, how you intend to get there, and how the individuals on the team will contribute to the journey.

Mission Drives Culture

> *Culture is not just one aspect of the game – it's the game.*
> *In the end, an organization is nothing more than the*
> *collective capacity of its people to create value.*
> LOU GERSTNER, JR.

Crafting and sustaining a memorable organizational culture is not easy and does not happen overnight. Many organizations plow forward with tactical execution of things like celebrations and free food for all.

Know When Your Culture Is Failing

Despite these actions, many totally overlook the signs that their culture may be failing. I have highlighted some undeniable signs that organizational culture is on the downturn and there is minimal connection to the organizational mission or vision.

Employees Don't Trust Leaders

The leader sets an example, whether in the Army or in civilian life. The other people in the organization take their cue from the leader, not from what the leader says, but what the leader does.

COLIN POWELL

This is the reality for many organizations. Unfortunately, employees feel powerless when working with leaders they do not trust. Here is the thing: When leaders believe in and behave in line with organizational values and norms, the passion shines through. Then, the rest of the organization can follow.

Employees lose that trust and desire to follow as soon as the leader's integrity is compromised, because the frontline now feels a sense of betrayal.

As Colin Powell alludes to above, it is what leaders do or fail to do that nurtures a strong trust foundation. Trust is the bedrock for any positive and magnetic culture. A positive culture fails without it.

Try to do everything you can do to build trust with your people. It will provide the fuel for a winning culture.

Employees Don't Feel Valued

The role of a creative leader is not to have all of the ideas; it's to create a culture where everyone can have ideas and feel that they're valued.

KEN ROBINSON

I spend a lot of time meeting and sitting down with frontline employees during focus groups. The one common thread I hear is a pride in being able to voice their opinion during the focus group. I get a real sense that they don't often feel heard. In fact, the very sad state is that many organizational leaders actually ask their employees for feedback, but then do nothing about what they hear.

That is even worse.

By asking for ideas but never either implementing ideas or letting them know why you decided to go in a different direction, you erode their desire to contribute creative ideas.

What if you contributed valuable energy to innovate on a particular project and then they decided not to move forward without a word? I would feel deflated, because I would think that I wasted my energy. Value your people's opinion and voice. Empower them to think outside of the box to maintain an innovative culture.

There Is No Alignment

While the other two signs are sad to witness, there is nothing more painful than a lack of organizational alignment.

What do I mean by this?

When no one agrees on how everyone should behave in relation to one another, when employees get mixed messages from different members of leadership. When the senior team has different ideas about direction, but continues to focus on the tactical side of the business.

This can be a very confusing time for managers, supervisors, and their teams who are looking for inspiration and a clear direction. They want to know what they are working towards. Culture is negatively impacted when there is no clear sense of organizational unity.

Fundamentally, positive organizational cultures stem from organizations full of trust, where employees feel valued for what they contribute, and when the mission, vision, values, and norms are adopted by all. Once we remove any of these necessary elements, we will not be able to sustain a winning culture.

Be Purposeful To Bring Mission And Vision To Life

Recently, I had a great conversation with an enlightened leader of an organization that is already doing quite well. She recalled for me that her large team is known for being the "poster child" of excellence and performance within the much larger organization. Nonetheless, she did not want to rest on their laurels. Instead, she wanted to be more purposeful in creating a positive culture. The promising thing about this leader is that she is self-aware and owns that she drives the culture of her team. I am pumped to work with such a forward-thinking person, because I feel like my counsel makes a difference.

You see, organizations that are renowned for their culture do not leave it to chance. They do culture on purpose, by setting a vision that moves the organization to do great things.

What do I mean?

Here are the main ways they do culture on purpose and create deep connections to organizational mission:

They Take Time To Dream And Codify

It is critical to figure out what type of organization you want to be and the culture you want to have before plunging into tactical execution. When I refer to "dreaming," I mean that we must first think about the possibilities. Do you think Disney's special culture was born from just tactics? That is not likely.

What are the non-negotiable components of the perfect culture for your organization?

Make sure to write down your thoughts. Disseminate an outline of your thoughts. Create a diary of your culture dreams to make you capture the essence properly. Don't let reality get in the way of dreaming big!

They Include More People In The Planning

I cannot highlight this point enough. Do not set out to transform your organization's culture all alone.

First, try to gather feedback and insights from your managers. Then seek out frontline input. Remember, everyone needs to be vested in this new direction. This was another thing I admire about the enlightened leader I referred to before. She wanted to involve a much larger team in the culture discussion.

It's just plain good business to use the voices of those who have to work in the culture to transform it. Maybe you can form a culture team. Have some fun, and dream with the masses.

They Focus On Getting The Right People In The Right Places

Arguably, this step is the key to a successful culture transformation. If you have the right frontline teams but misaligned managers to lead them, you will have a hard time on a culture journey.

If your leaders are in it for themselves and are not people who are other-centered, cultural transformation will fail.

Aligning the right people in the right places and ensuring they are on board with your new direction is critical to your success. This is a key element of doing culture on purpose.

They Know That They Must Emulate And Innovate

In the culture space, organizational leaders want to be innovative. Often, they want to do it bigger and better than their competition. Sometimes, we can innovate by just emulating, with our own twist. Keep an open mind. Research organizations that you admire. Present those ideas to the culture team. Then allow other organizations' successes to fuel your new vibrant culture. Do you think that Zappos created its culture reputation out of thin air? No. It took purposeful action. Ideas are right in front of us. Be open to emulate and innovate.

They Make Hard Decisions And Focus On The Good Of The Whole

This is a hard one. Organizations with very strong and positive cultures make hard decisions for the good of the whole on purpose. An example of this might be removing a key leader from the organization, because he or she is thwarting transformation. Perhaps the leader's values and actions are not in lockstep with a positive team-focused culture.

Regardless, strong leaders make hard decisions, especially when failing to do otherwise negatively affects the entire organization.

Don't be afraid to step out on the ledge to make sure everyone honors your organization's norms, values, and beliefs. Hopefully, your organization will
be one of those coveted places that others respect and want to emulate.

CONNECTION TO COWORKERS

In their 2015 Employee Engagement Report, TINYpulse discovered that peers are the number one thing people loved about their job. Nonetheless, in their 2017 Employee Engagement report they found that only 26% of employees felt connected to their peers (11% less than 2016), and this gap is causing cross-functional friction.

Think about it. We spend a minimum of 40 hours per week with our coworkers. We are bound to find friends there. Because we do spend so much time with them, they begin to feel like family. Just like we long to know and connect with our family, employees long to connect with their coworkers. Often, they make work enjoyable.

As TINYpulse's 2017 report revealed, a mere 27% of employees believe their organization's team-building efforts are sufficient. This is a severe oversight.

Organizations that create focused opportunities for coworkers to leverage their skills, passion, and knowledge in a cross-functional way to solve the business' greatest challenges are those that will win the loyalty game.

Connection To The Work That They Do

57% of employees said "meaningful work" contributes most toward a positive workplace sentiment.

Treat employees like they make a difference and they will.

JAMES GOODNIGHT, CEO, SAS

Whether it is a prospective candidate or a current employee, and yes, this might seem really obvious, communicate and include!

Don't leave anything to assumptions. You know what they say about assumptions! The best way to make prospective and current employees feel involved and appreciated is to share where the organization is today and where it is headed tomorrow. Don't just do it during the hiring process and then never again. Don't just talk about it once a year in some newsletter and never again.

I was recently talking to a client's team member, and he disclosed that he heard in passing that the company had made a major strategy change without informing the entire organization. The team member was baffled by this, because he felt that he was not important enough to be "in the know." Also, he felt that the team would be able to get behind the new direction in a way that could actually serve as a catalyst for faster growth.

How could this have been done differently?

CONTRACT REINFORCEMENT

Before professing a change in process, strategy, or culture, let your people know about it. Explain the reasons for the change. Let them know how they will play an important part. Everyone wants to feel important. Make it your business to find ways to communicate and include your employees in the change you want to see. They will buy into that change much faster!

SHOW THEM HOW TO MAKE A DIFFERENCE

People want to make a difference. We all want to feel that the work that we do is meaningful to us and the world around us.

Many organizations have embraced some level of social responsibility for a variety of reasons, not the least of which is to be more competitive. In fact, these days, when an organization has not taken that step to extend itself outside of itself for the benefit of the community, prospects and employees alike begin to question whether they want to be associated at all.

Organizations that provide opportunities for their people to help others in their community and truly make their mark are the ones who will fulfill that deep desire.

CONTRACT REINFORCEMENT

Evaluate whether you might be the driving force behind the lack of greatness. Perhaps you might consider 360 feedback for yourself and the entire leadership team, because it can be an invaluable exercise to get you and your organization back on track.

LAW #6

MAKE TEAMWORK THE FOCUS

"Managers account for at least 70% of variance in employee engagement scores across business units. When it comes to engaging employees and meeting their needs, great managers can be the key to unlocking high performance."

GALLUP, BUSINESS JOURNAL, APRIL 2015

THE TEAM IS THE TEAM

As the quote above clearly states, managers truly do hold the keys to employee engagement, which also directly impacts business results to include growth and customer retention. Getting your manager selection, promotion, and development right will make all the difference in creating a differentiated customer experience. There is no escaping it. Managers also mediate team dynamics.

A little while back, I watched 42 with my family, which is based on the true story of Jackie Robinson's triumphs and tribulations. At one point in the movie, the coach from the opposing team repeatedly taunted Jackie while he was up to bat and used racial slurs. Jackie knew that to continue on with the team and in the sport, he had to keep his mouth shut. In all previous instances of this type of taunting, Jackie's teammates sat silent, but in this case, one of his teammates jumped in for his defense. Shortly after that scene, and following many scenes of racism and rejection, one of Jackie's teammates talked to him out in the field and put his arm around him as the crowds looked at them in disgust. Jackie said, "What do you think you are doing?" His teammate replied, "You're on my team. What the hell am I supposed to do. Plus, my family is up there and I want them to see what I am made of."

In one other scene, one of Jackie's teammates, who was obviously wishing Jackie's demise, was traded to the same team where the coach was treating Jackie without dignity. The owner, played by Harrison Ford, decided to take a stand and fight for Jackie's right to be on the field and in the sport. The struggle that Jackie outwardly experienced with the racist opposing coach is one that often takes place between employees and their managers. Employees feel helpless to defend against the power of the boss. What the owner displayed in this case was his belief that those teammates who were not onboard to support everyone on the team equally sometimes go home.

Once his vision was defined, he decided to hire and fire based on it.

Not long ago, I managed a team of customer-facing team members while also leading a massive customer experience transformation effort. For the most part, everyone worked well together and supported one another in everything. There was one team member, however, who held negative feelings towards one of the other teammates for no obvious reason, but really did treat her badly, doing things like bringing gifts for everyone on holidays and leaving her out, not saying good morning in response to a greeting from this teammate, and not recognizing anything that this teammate did as positive.

Because I deeply believe in the power of team and that its unified existence makes any environment ripe for positive cultural improvements, I sat with my begrudging team member to see if I could get to the bottom of why she did not appear to like and want to support her other teammate. She did not confide in me the actual reason, but did confirm that she did not really care for her. I then let her know that a positive team dynamic was important to me, and that I needed her to try harder to become an authentic member of the team. She agreed that she would try. I gave her the benefit of the doubt

---

CONTRACT REINFORCEMENT

Have you taken the time to understand your true power as a manager? Do you own it with humility and respect the role you play in creating an engaged workplace? Managers define team cohesiveness. Take time to evaluate whether you are willing to take an unpopular position for the benefit of the entire team. Write down what might complicate this from happening and the benefit to doing so.

LEAVE A LEGACY FOR THE TEAM

I was recently listening to one of Zig Ziglar's books. He spoke of the importance of leaving a legacy or making our mark in the world. He spoke of legacy as significance. I often think about this in the context of work.

How can we all be purposeful in leaving a positive legacy in our workplaces?

Choose To Be Positive

We can complain because rose bushes have thorns, or rejoice because thorn bushes have roses. Abraham Lincoln

I have worked in organizations with good cultures and I have labored in somewhat toxic cultures as well, but the one thing that made work life easier for me was my attitude.

Whether good or bad, we all have the ability to choose to remain positive and optimistic despite our environment. I know that this is often easier said than done. However, I have found that those who are consistently positive have a reputation for uplifting those around them. Their legacy is helping others see the "roses" everywhere!

Choose To Give Without Getting

The value of a man resides in what he gives
and not in what he is capable of receiving.
ALBERT EINSTEIN

When we think of men and women in history who have left a legacy on the multitudes, we often realize that those individuals were "givers" in every sense of the word. Some examples include Anne Frank, Mother Theresa, Martin Luther King, Jr., and Zig Ziglar. All chose to give to others first without a definite reciprocity.

They were smart enough to know, as I once Mary Kay Ash said:, "What you put into the lives of others comes back into your own."

Some of my most memorable learning came from taking part in employee-led training on topics in their areas of expertise. Each time, I remember thinking about how wonderful it is that they chose to share their knowledge and gifts with others to help us all get better. They gave of themselves.

Those who leave the deepest legacies at work and in our world do so by giving first and receiving last. Go about your day seeking to give. It will feel much better and take you a long way.

Choose To Think BIG

Especially when it comes to the potential that lies within the people with whom you work.

I am sure many of you can relate to this one. Have you ever worked for or with someone who always saw the best in you?

Someone who knew you could achieve great things even when you doubted yourself?

Will you ever forget that special person?

Probably not.

When we choose to think of the big possibilities that exist within the people around us, we create a synergy and an energy that can fuel the stars!

Personally, I can think of examples of when I operated in this capacity and how much more bonded I was with the people with whom I worked.

Here's the cool part: Anyone can make this choice. This is not just for the manager or supervisor. Looking for the positive in our coworkers makes our journey that much better. Heck, it might even make us love our jobs!

SILOMANIA IS THE ENEMY

*Only by binding together as a single force
will we remain strong and unconquerable.*

CHRIS BRADFORD

When you think of the most memorable people with whom you have
ever worked, do you think of them as team players?

Personally, I have always embraced the idea that teams are much stronger
when they realized they were interconnected.

The weakest organizations are filled with people who are pursuing their
individual passions without concern for the good of the whole.

For me, the most memorable teammates were those who put the needs of
the team or organization ahead of their own. In fact, I would venture to
say that teammates who hold the philosophy of "me" are not respected at
all and would be voted off of the team if the opportunity presented itself.

A silo is a "system, process, department, etc. that operates in isolation
from others." Isolation means that you are alone.

Has there ever been a time in your life when you felt isolated from the
world, or you did not feel connected to anything outside of yourself? If
so, did you feel like you were motivated to do anything other than what
was best for yourself? It is highly likely that you suffered from what I call
"silomania."

Organizational silos are the enemy of teamwork. The reason why they are
so disruptive is that people cannot understand one another's strife if they
do not spend time with one another. They are unable to see how they
can work together to overcome business issues or to innovate, because
they become too bogged down in their departmental baggage. This is the
silomania mindset.

Over my years of working, I can think of only one or two times when I
worked in an organization that did not suffer from the silomania. Many
times, managers and leaders are focused on goals and initiatives in their

respective areas. They become advocates for their causes, but not for the organization as whole. Often, it is about saving their own skin or preserving their own bonuses. I remember one leader who controlled who received bonuses and at what amounts. This leader took more time coming up with reasons why one person or team did not deserve a certain bonus over another person or team. It was whatever served this leader best.

Instead, what if this leader looked to align objectives that promoted team goals and collaboration instead of promoting divisive decision-making? I would venture to guess that the leader's bonuses would be much bigger and the organization would be healthier for it.

I have found myself protecting my turf from time to time out of fear that someone would undermine my efforts. I had to change my mindset to focus on the good of the larger team. I even remember one of my managers calling me out in a meeting to continue the silomania mindset. It drove her nuts that I would not take part. Instead, I chose to focus on the customers and how what they wanted aligned with the entire organization. This drove her nuts, but I was not giving into the silomania mindset.

CONTRACT REINFORCEMENT

Rid your organization of silomania by working more in collaborative environments. Think about how the physical spaces in your workplace promote teamwork, or foster silomania. Create cross-functional teams when looking to innovate or solve organizational issues. Jot down the one way you can stop silomania in its tracks inside your organization.

LAW #7

PAY THEM EQUITABLY

While many of us will never earn the types of signing bonuses and multi-million-dollar contracts that the top picks in the NFL make, we all expect to be paid what we are worth.

Of course, this is relative to job type, location, skills, experience and education. Nonetheless, employees are looking to land at a place where they feel not only that they can start at a fair and competitive pay, but that they can experience periodic increases in the form of performance bonuses.

In some cases, it may be difficult to give away more of the pie, especially if you are a smaller organization. Think creatively! Offer other intangibles that do not require a significant outlay of resources.

Your pennies will be well spent!

CREATE AN ENVIRONMENT OF WORK-LIFE INTEGRATION

- 82% of employees say they would be more loyal to their employers if they had flexible work options.
- 38% of employees cite work responsibilities and 30% cite work/life balance as leading contributors to their loyalty.
- 22% of people have changed jobs due to work/life balance issues.
- Nearly 40% of employees said they wished their employer cared more about their work/life balance.

I have four young children. They are my treasures. I work for them, not to get away from them. In my working career, I was much more likely to stay longer with an organization if it allowed me either flexibility in location of work or hours of work. My feeling was that if the organization for which I worked cared enough about the things I needed to be able to care for my family, then I would be more committed to meeting the organization's needs for a longer period of time.

It appears both employers and employees may have work to do in 2015 to address pay inequality or wage gaps between men and women, as three in five employees (62%) do not believe men and women are paid equally. This differs significantly by gender, as 75% of women do not believe men and women are paid equally, compared to just half (50%) of men.

Just 37% of engaged employees would consider leaving for a 20% raise or less, compared to 54% of actively disengaged employees.

Are you paying your top talent what they are worth?

PAY THEM A FAIR WAGE

It is more profitable in the long term to minimize employee turnover and maximize employee productivity, commitment and loyalty.

CRAIG JELINEK, CEO, COSTCO

HAPPY EMPLOYEES, HAPPY CUSTOMERS
(COSTCO 2015/2016 case study)

Though the physical plant might be spartan, the way Costco treats its employees is anything but. At a time when many retailers are cutting staff and reducing employee hours to cut costs and avoid paying benefits, Costco is an anomaly. It sees employees as an asset to be respected and invested in, not as a cost to be minimized. Former CEO Jim Sinegal once told Stores magazine, "We've always had the attitude that if you hire good people, provide good jobs, good career opportunities, and good wages, good things will happen in your business."

Current CEO Jelinek has learned well, and added the consumer into the equation. In 2013 Jelinek wrote to Congress urging an increase in the federal minimum wage for the first time since 2009. "We know it's a lot more profitable in the long term to minimize employee turnover and maximize employee productivity, commitment and loyalty." He was also quoted as saying, "It also puts more money back into the economy and creates a healthier country."

Costco pays its employees an hourly average that is more than two and a half times the minimum wage, and almost twice what Walmart employees make. Almost 80 percent of its employees have company-sponsored health insurance. With initiatives such as these, Costco earns incredible employee loyalty, which in turn results in fantastic productivity.

At Price Club, Sol marked everything up a small flat amount because he felt retailers added only limited value to the consumer purchase equation. He also believed firmly in treating employees, customers, and vendors with respect—and in the process, rewarding shareholders. When Sinegal brought the Price Club model to Seattle in 1983 to start Costco, then merging the two and going public in 1995, Wall Street repeatedly begged the retailer to reduce wages and health benefits. Instead, Sinegal, in a nod to his former boss, increased benefits and wages every year, including during the recession. The company's attitude was "the economy is bad; we should figure out how to give people more."

To preserve the company culture, it prefers to grow executives from within rather than hiring business school graduates. The many MBAs working at the company earned their degrees while working there. Said Sinegal: "Culture isn't the most important thing; it's the only thing."

Despite the sagging economy and challenges to the industry, Costco paid its hourly workers an average of $20.89 an hour in 2016, not including overtime (vs. the minimum wage of $7.25 an hour). Eighty-eight percent of Costco employees have company-sponsored health insurance. Costco workers with coverage pay premiums that amount to less than ten percent of the overall cost of their plans. It treats its employees well in the belief that a happier work environment will result in a more profitable company. "I just think people need to make a living wage with health benefits," says Jelinek. "It also puts more money back into the economy and creates a healthier country. It's really that simple."

Costco proves that organizations can get rich by employing an employee-first strategy.

In its 2015 Engagement Report, TINYpulse found that one out of every four team members is willing to leave if your competitor gives them a better offer.

Below are a few factors they uncovered that drive their willingness to leave in some employee's own words:

- **Life circumstances:** "Due to my current financial situation, I would have to seriously consider it. I struggle living paycheck to paycheck even with overtime pay. Honestly, I don't see the possibility of getting a 10% raise with this company."

- **Lack of appreciation:** "I would leave not just for the raise but for just positive feedback from supervisors. It seems that some supervisors feel that they need to point out everything wrong but do not balance it with what you accomplish. So all the hard work seems for naught."

- **Lack of competitive salaries:** "Based on what I've heard from employees at competitors/other companies in the space, they are making significantly more with additional perks. It's hard not to listen to those types of comments."

SUMMING UP THE CENTS

There are myriad of ways to pay an employee equitably in line with the psychological contract. Remember, employees want to feel safe and cared for when they agree to work for an employer. When an employer commits to use its resources to ensure that their employees can pay for their most basic needs, they feel safer and more willing to stay longer.

Aside from a more flexible schedule, providing a strong benefit offering, or even equity in the organization will go a long way to attracting and retaining top talent. Some organizations even offer cool perks like free food, which can add to the bottom line for employees.

Offering work-life balance options, paying fair wages, creating access to strong benefits and equity and other creative perks are all things that add up to paying employees equitably. Equitable pay is not the number one reason employees remain loyal to an organization, but it is still an important factor.

CONTRACT REINFORCEMENT

Do you ever gauge whether your workforce perceives that you pay them equitably? Do you dive deep into what they think is fair? Don't sidestep the issue. Have the courage to face this head on. This bravery will speak volumes about your commitment to them and their sense of safety. Incorporate a question about pay equity into your next employee survey and make sure to allow them to state details.

CONCLUSION

MAKING OR BREAKING THE CONTRACT

In this highly competitive talent acquisition and talent management environment where employees are being courted by "sexier" employers, organizations that focus on the details around the relationship with their employees will have a clear competitive advantage. This advantage solidifies the psychological contract that is entered into at the beginning of any employer/employee relationship.

Before I close this chapter of our journey together, I want to share a case study that is close to me and is still evolving.

THE PSYCHOLOGICAL CONTRACT IN ACTION

A very close friend of mine decided to leave her current employer for another organization. It wasn't a very hard decision except for the fact that she is a very loyal person and one who refuses to fail.

From the beginning of her relationship with her almost former employer, I was stunned by how much they made her feel unwanted, not a part of the team, with very little hope of professional development. Were they the most horrible employer out there? No, not likely.

What stands out, though, is not what they didn't do, but what the competing employer did do.

FOCUS ON THE DETAILS

Employees interact with an organization even before the decision to apply has been made.

Many organizations fail to take the time to ask employees about how they experience the organization. Then they don't take the necessary steps to frame out the best possible journey for future or current employees by taking their voices into account.

It was clear to me that my friend's soon-to-be employer took some very clear, well-thought-out steps to create an amazing experience for its prospective recruits and new employees.

Their employee experience was no accident. They spared no detail.

Here are some great things they did before she even started her first day on the job, but after she accepted the offer:

- Signed her up for professional memberships
- Arranged and fully paid for a trip for her to attend a renowned conference with access to premier client entertainment activities and budget
- Sent her a form for her to fill out to make sure her business cards would look exactly like she envisioned, so that they would be available to her on her first day
- Sent her an equipment request form to make sure she had everything she needed, down to what type of cell phone she needed, computer hardware and type, etc.
- Asked her if she had any other concerns and whether she could think of any other issues about which they had not thought
- Confirmed that her travel reservations conformed to what was necessary for her family

At some point, my friend started to think, "Is this too good to be true? They are waiting on me hand and foot."

BE EQUITABLE WITH THE EXPERIENCE

One of the things her new firm did was to book a beautiful suite at the conference where clients could come to mix and mingle with the firm's brightest. This would be by invitation only, of course, and my friend was thrilled to be able to invite a few of her best clients in for a peek.

She told me that when she invited one key client to this lovely VIP event, the customer said, "It doesn't surprise me that they are doing this. For the last few years, your firm has really focused on the experience they offer to customers, including their marketing, quality of sponsorships, and other offerings. Pretty impressive."

My friend thought, "It is impressive! They are doing the same with me!"

Shortly after this exchange with the client, the hiring manager at her soon-to-be employer sent her an email stating that she was so excited that my friend was coming aboard and looked forward to working with her. The hiring manager let her know that she had organized a small team to handle the marketing for her practice. She had arranged for professional pictures to be taken while she was in the corporate office. Finally, she told my friend that the leadership team would be taking her to lunch on her first day. After all of this, my friend confessed that she finally felt valued and important.

She felt free to do her job without distraction. Her new employer's service focus and reputation is out in the universe for customers and employees alike. Their market presence is hard to beat.

She admitted that the way she was being treated by her almost-former employer is not horrible, but that this new firm is so far ahead.

The differences really stood out.

All of their doing what they said they would do and following up frequently to let her know next steps were worlds apart from her almost-former employer, and, to be honest, any other employer experience she has ever had.

Before she was hired on at her almost-former employer, the hiring manager talked a good game, but the culture did not line up to meet it.

AFTER THE HONEYMOON

I have stayed in close contact with her since she took her new role well over a year ago. The picture is not all rosy and bright. Once the courting period stopped, reality kicked in and so did the poor treatment. She worked extensive hours and the issue of the bonus never came up until she broached it. She was promised one, but she had to fight tooth and nail to get it. She recalled for me that "it was not a horrible place, but there was an awkwardness." She asked me how organizations can create an environment where employees enjoy their workplaces so much that their last day they wish was their first day. How do we create a sense of belonging and build a nurturing environment?

Here are some small steps to put in place after onboarding:

- Make sure they have all of the office supplies they need on day one.

- Provide them help with login and phone set up.

- Give directions to local restaurants (survival kit). A while back, a coworker called me when I first started a job to welcome me and let me know what was around the area to eat. She left an impression on me.

- Build in a process for a check-ins to make sure you are meeting their needs.

- Don't be afraid of the feedback. Ask where you are falling short.

- After they have been working there 6-12 months, make sure to check in to see if they have taken any vacation time. Are you creating an environment that makes it impossible?

- Have you checked in to gauge whether they need staff support or anything else?

THE REALITY OF THE CONTRACT

About a year with the same firm, my friend reported that she felt more secure in her role. Her compensation model was not very clear, but they took some steps to meet her halfway. The biggest benefit she received was autonomy to decide when to work and when she might need to focus on home. She no longer felt like she was walking on eggshells.

She admitted that because they dropped the ball after onboarding and on some compensation issues, she did not feel totally loyal, but because they gave her a chance to shine in other areas she felt more loyal than she did to her previous employer. Even though the journey was not completely smooth, she confessed that her manager showed her more deference and respect and included her in organizational changes. This collaboration and support has made the difference.

During her time with this employer, she received other job offers. While they were tempting, her current manager's increased communication and actions taken to meet my friend's needs made her more loyal. She is not likely to leave anytime soon.

THE FINAL CLAUSE

In this book, I set out to share the 7 Intuitive Laws of Employee Loyalty through a series of stories and case studies. In a world where employees have more choices than ever of where and how to work and earn a living, organizational leaders must take the issues of employee engagement and loyalty to heart.

I chose these Laws, because they are the most prominent reasons why employees report being loyal or disloyal to their employers. There are organizations that understand that change is necessary to get different results. First, though, it starts with a mindset. Organizations that take the psychological contract seriously and live out their implicit agreement with their employees will bear true fruit from employee loyalty Remember, people are loyal to the people inside of organizations. They are not loyal to buildings or legal entities.

I have come full circle in my place in this world. While I am not a practicing attorney, I am proud to say that I am an advocate for those who don't often have a voice. I used my experience, insights and empathy to reveal the powerlessness that employees often feel. I, too, felt this way at times in my life. My hope for all leaders or prospective leaders who read this is that you commit to being the person your team members value and desperately need.

Cheers to you for a fruitful and growth-filled journey!

REFERENCES

INTRODUCTION

Adkins, A. (2016, April 13). *US Employee Engagement Reaches New High in March.* Retrieved from gallup.com

Dvorak, N. and Kruse, William E. (2016, March 29). *Managing Employee Risk Requires a Culture of Compliance.* Retrieved from gallup.com

Temkin, Bruce (2015) *Employee Engagement Benchmark Report.* Retrieved from e-junkie.com/temkingroup/product

Beck, R. and Harter, J. (2014, March 25). *Why Great Managers Are So Rare.* Retrieved from gallup.com

Adkins, A. (2016, May 12). *Millennials: The Job-Hopping Generation.* Retrieved from gallup.com

Borysenko, K. (2015, April 22). *What Was Management Thinking? The High Cost of Employee Turnover.* [Web log post]. Retrieved May 26, 2017, from eremedia.com

Hoffman, Reid, Ben Casnocha, and Chris Yeh. *The Alliance: Managing Talent in the Networked Age.* Boston, MA: Harvard Business Review, 2014. Print.

LAW #1

Harter, J. and Adkins, A. (2015, April 2). *What Great Managers Do to Engage Employees.* [Web log post]. Retrieved May 26, 2017, from hbr.com

Rigoni, B. and Nelson, B. (2016, February 5). *The No-Managers Organizational Approach Doesn't Work.* Retrieved from gallup.com

LAW #2

McQuaid, M. (2015, March 6). *Employee Appreciation Day Study Shows Best Way to Thank Employees is to Recognize What They Do Best.* Retrieved from Businesswire.com

Davis, K. (2016, April 2). *Reward and Recognition: What's Really Driving Employee Engagement and Career Advancement.* [Web log post]. Retrieved January 2, 2017, from bamboohr.com

Employee Engagement and Organizational Culture Report with New 2016 Addendum. Seattle. TINYpulse

Mulder, P. (2015). *McClelland Motivation Theory.* Retrieved [February 1, 2017] from ToolsHero: https://www.toolshero.com/effectiveness/mcclelland-motivation-theory/

Alton, C. and Gostick, A. (2007) *The Carrot Principle.* Simon and Schuster. New York.

LAW #4

Huskin, K. (2015, March 11). *Two-Thirds of Managers Need Guidance on How to Coach and Development Careers.* Retrieved from right.com

Balancing Employer and Employee Priorities, (2016, July). Andorra, Argentina, Australia, Towers Watson

Adkins, A. (2015, April 2). *Only 35% of U.S. Managers Are Engaged in Their Jobs.* Retrieved from gallup.com

Bronstein, Stacy (2015, August 12). *One in Three Employees Claim to Have a Job Rather Than a Career.* [Web Blog post] Retrieved March 25, 2017 on mercer.com

Employee Engagement and Organizational Culture Report with New 2016 Addendum. Seattle. TINYpulse

LAW #5

MacPherson, D. (2015, July 20). *10 Things You Need to Know About Employee Engagement.* [Web blog post] Retrieved February 3, 2017 on modernsurvey.com

Employee Engagement Report. The Broken Bridges of the Workplace. (2017) Seattle. TINYpulse

Employee Engagement and Organizational Culture Report with New 2016 Addendum. Seattle. TINYpulse

Casserly, M. (2013, January 2). *Top Five Reasons Employees Will Quit in 2013.* Retrieved from Forbes.com

LAW #6

Namely (2016, June 14). *Forget perks and gimmicks, research shows employees want improvements to core HR and benefits first.* Retrieved from PRnewswire.com

Beck, R. and Harter, J. (2014, March 25). Why Great Managers Are So Rare. Retrieved from gallup.com

LAW #7

Lewis, R. (2016, February 16). *'Costcoholics': Costco's $113.7 Billion Addicts.* Retrieved from Forbes.com

Stone, B. (2013, June 7). *Costco CEO Craig Jelinek Leads the Cheapest, Happiest Company in the World.* Retrieved from bloomberg.com

DePillis, L. (2016, March 4). *Why Costco is Raising Its Minimum Wage for the First Time in Nearly a Decade.* [Web blog post] Retrieved from washingtonpost.com

Reynolds, B. (2015, August 25). *Survey: 76% Avoid the Office For Important Tasks.* [Web blog post] Retrieved from flexjobs.com

2016 Workplace Index. (2016) Staples Business Advantage

LABOR OF LOVE: What Employees Love About Work & Ways To Keep The Spark Alive. (2015) Virgin Pulse

Keener, B. (2013, March 5) *Costco, Eileen Fisher and Small Business Owners Nationwide Support Fair Minimum Wage Act Introduced Today In Congress.* [Web blog post] Retrieved by businessforafairminimumwage.org

Employee Engagement Report. The Broken Bridges of the Workplace. (2017) Seattle. TINYpulse

Glassdoor team, (2015, January 9). *More than 1 in 3 Employees Will Look For a Job in 2015 if They Do Not Receive a Pay Raise.* [Web blog post] Retrieved from glassdoor.com

Rigoni, B. and Nelson, B. (2016, January 15). *Retaining Employees: How Much Does Money Matter?* Retrieved from gallup.com